THE OTTOMAN EMPIRE

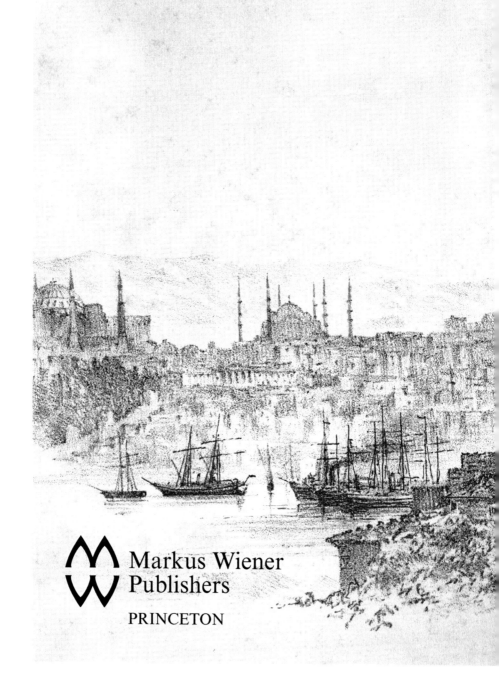

**Markus Wiener
Publishers**

PRINCETON

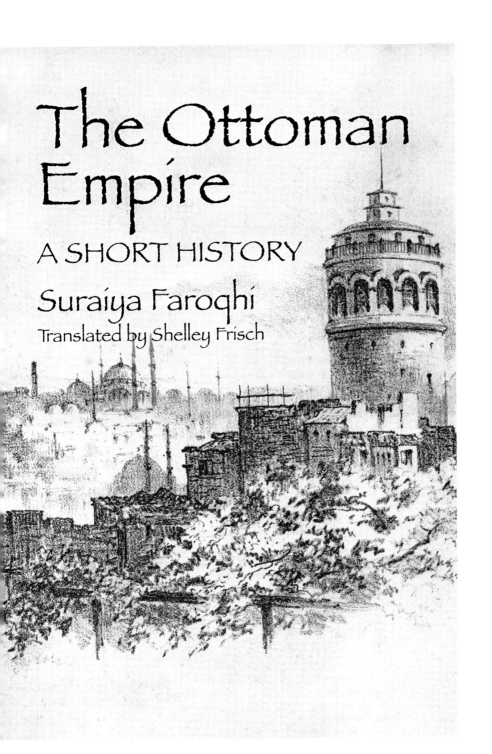

The Ottoman Empire

A SHORT HISTORY

Suraiya Faroqhi

Translated by Shelley Frisch

The translation of this work was supported by a grant from the Goethe-Institut,
which is funded by the Ministry of Foreign Affairs, Berlin.

For information, write to Markus Wiener Publishers
231 Nassau Street, Princeton, NJ 08542
www.markuswiener.com

Library of Congress Cataloging-in-Publication Data

Faroqhi, Suraiya, 1941-
  [Geschichte des Osmanischen Reiches. English]
  The Ottoman Empire : a short history / Suraiya Faroqhi ;
translation by Shelley Frisch.
    p. cm.
  Includes bibliographical references and index.
  ISBN 978-1-55876-448-4 (hardcover : alk. paper)
  ISBN 978-1-55876-449-1 (pbk. : alk. paper)
  1. Turkey—History—Ottoman Empire, 1288-1918.
  I. Frisch, Shelley Laura. II. Title.
  DR440.F3713 2008
  956'.015—dc22
  2008035506

Markus Wiener Publishers books are printed in the United States of America
on acid-free paper and meet the guidelines for permanence and durability
of the Committee on Production Guidelines for Book Longevity of the
Council on Library Resources

CONTENTS

v

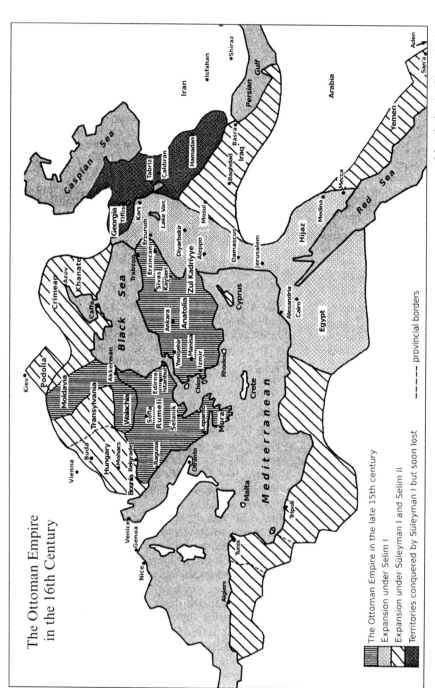

The Ottoman Empire
in the 16th Century

Map design by Sinan Çetin

The Ottoman Empire in the late 15th century

Expansion under Selim I

Expansion under Süleyman I and Selim II

Territories conquered by Süleyman I but soon lost

---- provincial borders

ACKNOWLEDGMENTS

Every book is a product of many people: as a first step after writing, the manuscript is read by the author's colleagues, who suggest changes and, most important, provide encouragement. I am especially grateful to Machiel Kiel, who upon reading the first German version of this text said that it was easy to criticize—but very difficult to provide a satisfactory account of Ottoman history in a small book. In the meantime, several reviews have appeared, and in spite of occasional dismay, I have benefited from them when producing the English version: more than a third of the present volume has been newly written. As for the translation, I am greatly indebted to Shelley Frisch. Furthermore, several synthetic works have appeared since 2000, and I have had the opportunity to learn a great deal, especially from Caroline Finkel's fine study.[1]

Other "food for thought" has come from my students in Munich and Istanbul, without whose questions and curiosities this text would never have been produced. In Munich, Yavuz Köse made it possible for me to write in spite of the bureaucratic distractions inherent in today's university systems; and the same thing must be said about Elektra Kostopoulou and Sinan Çetin in the History Department of Bilgi University in Istanbul. At a later stage of preparation, I had much help, particularly from Bill Blair, whose searching questions made me look into certain issues that I would otherwise have neglected. To all these people, and to my publisher, Markus Wiener, my heartfelt thanks. Of course, I am responsible for the many defects that doubtless remain.

PRONUNCIATION OF
TURKISH LETTERS

(From Geoffrey Lewis, *Turkish Grammar*
[Oxford: Oxford University Press, 1967], p. 1)

a	as in 'but'
c	as in 'jam'
ç	as in 'child'
e	as the first vowel in 'elder'
ğ	almost inaudible, between vowels
ı	as the 'a' in 'serial'
i	as in 'sit'
j	as in French 'jeune'
ö	as the first vowel in French 'jeune'
ş	sh
ü	as the 'u' in French

Introduction

After a long eclipse, empires are back in force as a topic of discussion, and a number of scholarly projects have been dedicated to the Roman, Chinese, Moghul, Spanish, Russian, and British empires both in their formal and informal versions – to say nothing of other varieties closer to home. The Ottoman Empire forms part of this select but still sizeable group of polities that claimed to govern if not the whole world, then at least a major part of it; and it now is receiving a certain amount of attention on the part of historians interested in comparative studies on empires and other topics. This inclusion of Ottoman history into a broader context in which it traditionally played no role is quite novel, and at least in part due to the large amount of archival documentation that has become accessible in recent years. The present book is meant to give an idea of why a student interested in the present-day Middle East, urbanism, global labor migration, or the history of women and the family might find research on the Ottomans to be of value.

Before we begin our discussion of the Empire's political, economic, social, and cultural history, it therefore makes sense to introduce the results of certain major studies that recently have enriched our field; they have for the most part been published during the last ten years or in some cases are even still in the dissertation stage. In the present introduction, we will begin with a discussion of the three hundred years that separate the conquest of Constantinople in 1453 (from now on: Istanbul) from the military, political, and economic crisis of the late 18th century. This period is called "modern" in Turkish historiography and corresponds to what is called "early modern" in the English-speaking world. These three hundred years will be the focus of attention here, as I believe that 19th- and 20th-century developments cannot be understood without taking the preceding

3

period into account. Afterwards, we will turn to a crop of new studies that deal with the "transition years" between the 1760s and the mid-19th-century restructuring of the Ottoman administration known as the Tanzimat. From there, we will proceed to some of the research that has been done on the Empire's final years. To round off the discussion, we will present a few major recent syntheses.

Legitimizing the Empire: Conquests and Instability in the Borderlands

How the Ottoman elites viewed their position in the world and legitimized the rule of the sultans has become a significant focus of scholarly attention. In the eyes of authors close to the sultans' court who wrote on these matters, the lands that made up the Empire possessed a special value. Praising their extent and qualities formed part of the legitimizing stance that sultans and their chroniclers broadcast to friend and foe. Already in the 16th century, the possession of Istanbul was regarded as a reason for assuming that God had endowed the sultans with a special grace; and when an Ottoman ambassador visited the Shah of Iran in the early 1720s, he also felt a need to emphasize the beauty of the sultan's capital in order to make the rival ruler aware of Ottoman glory.

In addition, the Ottoman elite saw itself as privileged in the sense that it claimed to govern the most important Sunni Muslim polity, which was at least in principle continually expanding. Delineating the borders of the empire was therefore problematic. While Istanbul, and during earlier centuries Bursa and Edirne (Adrianople), were the clearly defined centers, even in the later 1600s the northern and Mediterranean frontiers were still being extended, albeit at the expense of secondary European powers such as Venice and Poland. Well into the eighteenth century, the sultans thus regarded it as an important element of their role as legitimate rulers that they extended—and should be viewed as extending—the borders of the Muslim world. Of course, imperial propaganda did not exclude pragmatism:

for the most part the Ottoman elite were well aware of what was possible at any given time and took a practical approach when war and peace were at issue.

Ottoman expansion in Europe was a key feature when it came to legitimizing the sultan because this small continent was ruled and inhabited by "infidels." Throughout the 14th, 15th and early 16th centuries, the Ottoman armies advanced at a rapid pace: Balkan polities of the period were small and relatively unstable, and the few coalitions patched together by western European rulers to "roll back" the sultans' armies were all resounding failures. After the death of Süleyman the Magnificent (r. 1520-66), however, gains at the expense of the Habsburgs slowed down, and in the Long War of 1593-1606 were limited to a few fortresses. After all, even if we consider only the Vienna-based branch and leave out the mighty Spanish Habsburgs, the successors of Ferdinand I (1503-64) ruled an empire that could compete with that of the Ottomans. Unlike the princes of southeastern Europe, the Habsburgs were well entrenched in a large territory encompassing today's Austria, the Czech Republic, Slovakia, and a strip of Hungary, to say nothing of possessions farther west, for instance in Alsace. Moreover, while the title of Holy Roman Emperor did not convey a great deal of power, the Habsburgs of Vienna held this honor on a quasi-hereditary basis, and in wars against the Ottomans, they could raise troops from a variety of German princes on account of their imperial status. These factors all had a role to play in halting the advance of the sultans' armies and, in 1683, bringing about what was from the Ottoman viewpoint the disaster of the second campaign against Vienna.

As they developed during the 16th and 17th centuries, Ottoman-Habsburg relations meant that both sides regarded their borders as inherently unstable. Within extensive zones, frontier skirmishes were routine. Certainly the notion of delineated borders, defined by means of natural or man-made markers and agreed upon with some neighboring ruler, was known to sultans and viziers long before the Treaty of Karlowitz (1699), in which Mustafa II (r. 1695-1703) had to recognize the loss of Hungary. There were some treaties with the kings of Poland that even in the 1400s determined concrete borders; but as, according to Islamic law, the sultans could only conclude short- and medium-term agreements with non-Muslim rulers, these borders did not imply permanency: they were called into question come the next war.

Yet the sultans did conclude treaties that prescribed lengthy periods of peace even with their Habsburg opponents, twenty years being normal in the 1600s. What is more, the sultans typically abided by the agreements they concluded. This fact did not go unnoticed at the Iranian court: in the early 18th century an Ottoman envoy to the shah was made uncomfortable by a pointed reference to the recent Treaty of Passarowitz (1718), with the length of its duration a particular embarrassment. Once more work has been done on the poorly documented relations of the sultans with other Islamic rulers, we will be able to say more about the manner in which Ottoman claims to preeminence among Muslim empires were received abroad. At present this remains an open question.

Unstable borders were not limited to neighboring Christian polities. From our perspective, both the Ottomans and the Safawids who governed Iran between about 1500 and 1722 were Muslim rulers; but the two sovereigns concerned did not see each other in that light at all. On the contrary: while competing for territory in Iraq, Azerbaijan, and the Caucasus, neither side regarded its opponent simply as a political rival. Presumably encouraged by their respective rulers, Sunnite religious cum legal scholars in Istanbul and their Shiite counterparts in Isfahan did their level best to exacerbate the conflicts between the two varieties of Islam, proclaiming "the others" to be heretics who did not deserve to be recognized as Muslims. This aggressive stance explains how Ottoman sultans could so easily legitimize their campaigns in western Iran, which were numerous.

When waging wars against the Safawids, and not just in confrontations with Christian rulers, the Ottoman sultans thus asserted that they were constantly expanding the sphere of Sunni right belief and thereby of Islam. Tabriz was conquered several times, even though the Ottomans were never able to hold on to the city for more than a few months or years. Campaigns in the Caucasus, which in the 1500s and 1600s was also mainly an Iranian sphere of influence, were defended with the same argument. Furthermore, these wars produced material benefits in the form of numerous Georgian slaves, but that was not a matter that Ottoman chroniclers discussed in any detail.[1]

The northern borders presented further complications. From the late 1400s, the Black Sea was an Ottoman lake, as the Genoese had been driven out of their trading posts and the khans of the Crimea obliged to recognize Ottoman suzerainty. However, the latter remained semi-independent rulers; moreover, they were Sunnites. Thus in the Ottoman view they could engage in wars of their own against the "infidel" tsars, but more importantly, the Tatars were expected to supply advance forces for Ottoman campaigns in central Europe.

In the north, for a long time there was no fixed border: in these lands the Tatars conducted major raids that supplied the slave markets of Istanbul and Aleppo, and fought battles against Cossack freebooters whose raids in the early 17th century extended to the southern shores of the Black Sea. Sometimes these confrontations led to outright warfare against the Polish kings as rulers of the Ukraine and the Russian tsars, for in one way or another, the Cossacks had pledged allegiance to either one of these rulers. At least this was true most of the time; for in 1648 and again in 1668 a group of Cossacks instead decided to recognize the sultan as their overlord. A long spate of warfare in 1681 was concluded by an agreement with the Russian tsar that a broad swath of territory would remain empty and neither side would establish any settlements therein. In the 18th century, when the Tsars and their subjects were progressing southwards, the Ottomans accepted the great rivers that empty into the Black Sea as the borders with the Russian realm and concentrated on defending a set of major fortresses, currently the subject of archeological studies. However, as time went by and the sultans lost territory, the borders were moved to rivers lying farther to the west (Bug, Dnjestr, Prut). As for the Tatar domains, in 1783 they were annexed by the Tsarina Catherine II; and the last khan fled to Ottoman territory, where he was soon killed.

Last but not least, there were the southern borders. They are not well documented and consequently have attracted few researchers. Central Africa was of interest to the Ottomans only very intermittently, but there were some interactions with Kanem and Bornu in the late 16th century. As for the southern border of Egypt, Ottoman garrisons followed the Nile and established an outpost near the First Cataract. Excavations have brought to light earthenware pots filled with documents issued by local qadis, mainly in Arabic but also in Ottoman Turkish; a few soldiers came from faraway Hungary and Sofia.[2] Yet farther to the east, close to the Red Sea and the Indian Ocean, in the 16th and 17th centuries there was a province of Habeş (Abyssinia) that consisted of a strip of coastal land, the interior remaining under its own Christian king. The sultans' central administration at one point considered this territory important enough to attach to it the port of Jiddah on the Arabian Peninsula: thus access to the holy city of Mecca by sea was to be controlled ultimately by the governor of Habeş.[3]

However, Ottoman chroniclers have mostly ignored this remote outpost of the Empire, and as a result we do not know much about the circumstances under which the sultans' governors first established their rule in this province, and later withdrew from it. Somewhat more information, however, is available on the Ottoman presence in Yemen. The first conquest (1538) was soon reversed by local forces. But in 1568-71 another campaign, conducted by the Grand Vizier Sinan Paşa, who had also added Tunis to the sultans' realm, resulted in a renewed Ottoman domination that lasted slightly over half a century. However, it is unlikely that the governors residing in San'a and the tax collectors stationed in the Red Sea and Indian Ocean ports ever exercised a great deal of control over the mountainous hinterland. Yet the dues collected from Indian Ocean traders arriving in Yemen did give the administration access to quantities of pepper, which was in demand in the Ottoman lands just as much as in contemporary Europe. Moreover, the popularity of coffee, hitherto an Abyssinian and Yemenite specialty, rapidly increased throughout the sultans' territories in the second half of the 16th century – presumably the most enduring consequence of the Ottoman presence in these lands.

While the interior of the Arabian Peninsula remained outside the sultans' control, in the 16th century the Ottomans did establish a province on the eastern coast that they called al-Hasa or more often Lahsa. From here, trade links were formed to southern Iraq, where after the conquest of Baghdad by Sultan Süleyman in 1534 the Ottomans had placed a janissary garrison in the port city of Basra and formed a set of new provinces. However, holding on to Basra proved difficult, as the area was separated from Baghdad by a broad strip of marshland, whose inhabitants were never completely subdued. Even so, the garrison of Basra was supplied by river transport from remote Bire/Birecik on the Euphrates; but in the 17th century, the city came to be governed by a local dynasty that only nominally acknowledged the Ottoman sultans as their overlords.

In many cases, the Ottomans on the southern borders of their empire were confronted with Muslim rulers; and this fact made it more difficult to legitimize conquest. Quite often, these regions were too poor to support even the garrisons sent out to retain them in the sultans' orbit. Pragmatically speaking these "outposts of empire" were worth conquering and keeping because the soldiers stationed there could protect the resources of the inland provinces. Such postings seem to have been unpopular not only among soldiers in the sultans' service but also among their commanders.

Given this situation, legitimizing discourses included the protection that the Ottoman sultans accorded to Mecca and Medina, which in the 16th century were under threat from Portuguese attacks. This stance was of special importance in the case of Yemen and other parts of the Arabian Peninsula, where Ottoman documents highlighted, in addition to Portuguese "unbelievers," the threat of Safawid "heretics" and their spies. As the Zaydi Imam of Yemen was a Shiite, his rule presumably appeared illegitimate. In Abyssinia, the Ottomans supported a Muslim candidate to the throne against his Christian rival; religious considerations apart, a Christian monarch could count on Portuguese support.

In the southern as in the northern borderlands between 1450 and 1650, the Ottomans did not encounter solidly constituted polities like the Habsburg and Safawid Empires. None of the principalities that they confronted in these regions could have resisted the sultan's armies for very long if they had not been protected by two factors. On the one hand, the distances involved were enormous and routes of communication passed through seas and rivers that were unsafe for navigation, or else through deserts. As a result, Ottoman campaigns in the northern as in the southern frontier regions were extremely costly. On the other hand, these borderlands were, in the eyes of the Ottoman central administration, simply not valuable enough to justify spending enormous sums of money on armies and garrisons. Once the conquest was officially regarded as complete, the governors of the southern borderlands normally operated on minimal budgets, and as a result, local forces soon were given a chance to reassert themselves.

Lords of Two Seas?

Maritime borders were another source of instability, and in the Ottoman case, such borders were both numerous and lengthy. Yet among his many titles, Sultan Süleyman the Magnificent styled himself "lord of the Mediterranean and the Black Sea." In the south, the Indian Ocean was the limit, at least while the struggle with the Portuguese was going on during the first half of the 16th century, and in an attenuated form, as long as the Ottomans controlled Yemen, until 1636. After that, the ocean was rarely an official concern except insofar as Indian traders and pilgrims to Mecca arrived by that route. Yet Ottoman records concerning these people were usually put together not in Istanbul but in Cairo. We may thus say that the Indian Ocean was downgraded to a provincial concern. In the north, the Black Sea was surrounded by Ottoman territories, but control was less than perfect; for as we have seen, in the early 17th century the constant attacks of Cossack pirates from the no man's land between the great rivers made it necessary to fortify coastal towns in northern Anatolia and even guard the approaches to Istanbul.

    In Ottoman eyes, the most important maritime border was doubtless the Mediterranean. Why this sea should have been a border at all is worth some discussion; for by the late 1500s only the northwestern quarter of the lands bordering this great inland sea was not occupied by Ottoman provinces. Spain, France, and the Italian principalities jostled for possession of a rather limited strip of coastland. However this non-Ottoman shore happened to be the richest in terms of rainfall, a precondition for agriculture and thereby for manufacture and trade. As a result, the sultans' navy, in spite of its impressive successes, was not able to bottle up its Spanish and other opponents in their ports, or even to conquer Malta, an island that controlled the passage between the eastern and western sections of the Mediterranean (siege in 1565). Maritime borders thus remained permeable. Perhaps for this reason they were mostly ignored when it came to agreements with foreign sovereigns; whatever border arrangements were concluded concerned the Eurasian land mass.

Instability in the realm of maritime affairs further increased in the 1600s and 1700s, when the rulers of Algiers, Tunis, and Tripoli, while continuing to recognize the paramount position of the sultan, insisted on concluding their own treaties with foreign rulers. These claims to at least a limited sovereignty had serious practical consequences. Any arrangements providing for the protection of foreign ships which the sultans might have concluded were not honored by the captains of Algiers, Tunis, and Tripoli unless they had been confirmed by their own provincial councils. Some European governments were pragmatic about such matters and concluded multiple agreements. But others were not and threatened to cause diplomatic problems if their ships were robbed in spite of having signed treaties with the sultan. Viewed from a different angle, Ottoman rulers were concerned about the possible erosion of their sovereignty over provinces that could only be controlled by a navy whose access was limited to a few months during the summer season. They therefore put pressure on the administrations of the North African provinces, usually with at most moderate success.

In spite of these difficulties, the Ottoman Empire, like its Roman predecessor, depended on the political control of maritime routes.

Grains from the coastal regions of today's Bulgaria and Romania, purchased by officially recognized merchants under the tightest possible state control, fed the army, the navy, the court with its many servitors, and above all Istanbul, probably the largest city in Europe, at least in the 1500s. From north of the Black Sea there arrived clarified butter, while the coastlands adjacent to the Aegean Sea produced grapes, an important sweetener in an age when sugar was scarce and expensive. Therefore, it was only in the mid-17th century, when central control was no longer as absolute as it had been a hundred years earlier, that Izmir, previously just a large village adjacent to a landing scale, developed into a major international port.

The Core Provinces

When discussing an empire it makes sense to differentiate between core and border provinces; and members of the Ottoman elite also recognized this distinction. Since today's Turkey consists of Anatolia, the eastern section of Thrace, and Istanbul, a city of at least ten million straddling two continents, people often assume that these were the core regions of the Ottoman Empire as well. Yet this is not entirely true: the rule of the sultans expanded in southeastern Europe far more rapidly than in Anatolia. In 1521 Sultan Süleyman stood poised to invade Hungary, having taken the border fortress of Belgrade, in today's Serbia. Yet in the east-central parts of Anatolia, Ottoman rule during those very same years was not very secure, as the adherents of a certain local dynasty started a major rebellion in favor of their previous rulers.

We should therefore view the Ottoman Empire as spreading out from a center that included Bursa, Edirne, Salonika, and Istanbul as the major cities. After 1517, the Fertile Crescent became another basis of Ottoman power. Well into the 19th century, the Empire's core encompassed the regions to the west and east of the Aegean Sea as well as the provinces that make up today's Syria, Lebanon, Israel, and Palestine. Egypt had been a core province until the mid-1700s, but had lost that position well before Muhammad Ali Pasha established his vice-regal domain in the early 19th century. Creating a new core region in Anatolia thus was a 19th- and early 20th-century effort; and supplying Istanbul from this landlocked region became possible only after a certain number of railroads had been built.

Fostering Loyalty in Predominantly Christian Regions

How was this far-flung polity held together? Even though the sultans had achieved their position by conquest, it would be a mistake to assume that the empire was only maintained by military power. Ottoman forces in the inland provinces usually were quite small, garrisons numbering a few thousand men or, in smaller towns, no more than a few hundred. Moreover, the citadels of the interior were often allowed to decay; a 17th-century Ottoman traveler, when accounting for a decrepit fortification, might explain this situation by the simple statement that this or that town was far away from the frontiers. Heavily fortified places, by contrast, were typical of border zones such as eastern Anatolia and above all Hungary, where battles in the open field were rare; typically Ottoman and Habsburg military men fought for control of these fortresses. But border regions were not densely settled; therefore such concentrations of military power could not do "double duty" in securing the rule of the sultans.

This state of affairs is noteworthy especially if we keep in mind that large sections of the Balkan Peninsula remained Christian. King Philip II of Spain (r. 1556-98) knew what he was doing when, during the wars of his Vienna-based cousins with the sultans (1593-1606), he refused various suggestions to provoke uprisings in southeastern Europe. Religious concerns figured prominently among the reasons why most Balkan subjects of the sultans were not at all enthusiastic about coming under Habsburg domination; for both the Spanish and the Austrian branches of this dynasty were strongly committed to the Counterreformation, and thus made it state policy to enforce Catholic conformity among their subjects. As the majority of Balkan

Christians were Orthodox, and in Hungary and Transylvania Protestants of varying denominations were also quite numerous, we can explain why except under special circumstances, they were unlikely to prefer the Habsburg option. There were some exceptions, however, especially the commitment of Kosovo Serbs to the imperial cause during the 1680s and 1690s; in the end these people migrated to the Habsburg territories, where they found employment in the border militia.

The loyalties of Balkan subjects became more problematic once the 18th-century tsars of Russia, staunch promoters of Orthodoxy, developed territorial ambitions in the Balkans. But even then, the numerous incursions of Russian troops did not, for the most part, spark local anti-Ottoman rebellions. The one exception was the Peloponnesus in 1770, where Ottoman rule had previously been reestablished after a Venetian interlude and the new arrangements had resulted in a certain degree of local disaffection. Presumably Russian serfdom was a major deterrent: for while from the peasants' viewpoint Ottoman rule had its drawbacks, at least villagers were considered freemen and could often obtain legal redress from local qadis, or else by petitioning the sultan himself. Russian wartime taxation must also have contributed to the lack of enthusiasm among Balkan subjects of the sultans. It was mainly in crisis situations, such as during the Russo-Ottoman war of 1768-74, when unpaid soldiers ravaged the countryside of present-day Bulgaria that people who had been bankrupted by these attacks threw in their lot with the armies of the tsar: no taxation without protection.

On the positive side, Ottoman policy with respect to the Orthodox Church contributed materially to the stabilization of the regime. In all probability, the Ottoman government developed a certain partiality for this church in preference to other varieties of Christianity, if only because the spiritual heads of Orthodoxy were domiciled on the sultans' territory. For a long time it was assumed that the "millet system" which granted the recognized religious communities a considerable degree of judicial autonomy, was instituted in its entirety by Mehmed the Conqueror (r. 1451-81). Many scholars today question this view.

Arrangements in this early period were probably more ad hoc and much less formalized than they were to become in the 19th century; and the millets should rather be regarded as work in progress. In the 16th and 17th centuries judicial autonomy was in no way absolute: in spite of repeated condemnations by their men of religion, many Christians and Jews preferred to bring their disputes before the qadis.

But even so, the Orthodox Church had already become an integral part of the Ottoman tax-collecting machine by the 1500s: appointments to ecclesiastical dignities needed to be paid for, and bishops, metropolitans, and patriarchs recouped these payments to the Ottoman exchequer from their believers. As a result, these churchmen could be sure that the sultans would support them in case, for instance, members of their churches deserted them in favor of other denominations. Such support was forthcoming when in the 1700s and early 1800s Gregorian Armenians or Arab Christians of Aleppo decided to become Catholics – not that political pressures always sufficed to retain people within their established churches. But at the same time, the Orthodox Church which did not require elaborate training for most of its priests remained reasonably close to the faithful. This double involvement on the part of the church, with both ordinary believers and the sultans' governing apparatus, must have facilitated the integration of Orthodox believers within the Ottoman polity.

Integrating Local Elites

In provinces with Muslim and Christian majorities, establishing the Ottoman order meant integrating local elites. Only in exceptional cases such as Cyprus or Crete, where the Venetians and their close adherents either were killed in the fighting or else left the country, was this issue not of major importance; and even on these two islands, the Ottomans dealt with the Orthodox Church as a kind of local elite.

In the 15th and early 16th centuries a pattern emerged concerning the integration of Muslim territories: the sultans might at the beginning allow a member of the original princely family that had rallied to the Ottoman cause to govern as a kind of viceroy; or else they might chose their first governors from among this same dynasty.[4] At a later stage, descendants of such potentates still might be appointed as governors; but now they were sent to places far away from their fathers' or grandfathers' zones of influence, which by this time were governed as "regular" Ottoman provinces.

However, to this rule there were many exceptions; and after 1550 the pattern lost most of its validity. Now new conquests might be centrally governed from the outset, as happened in Cyprus and Crete, as well as in Podolia during the short-lived Ottoman annexation of the 1670s and 1680s. On the other hand, beginning in the late 1500s, provinces that had originally been closely controlled by the central administration, such as Tunis and Egypt, were dominated by local military men and sea captains who the authorities in Istanbul tolerated as long as they sent a certain amount of tribute and recruited some soldiers for the sultan's campaigns.

The most remarkable exception to the standardized process of centralization observed in earlier ages is surely that of the provinces which today make up Syria, Lebanon, Israel, and Palestine. These regions had all been part of the Mamluk sultanate. After 1516 the Ottoman government discontinued the importation of the military slaves, for whom the whole system had been named, and thus instituted a wholly new type of administration in the region. Yet while governors were appointed from Istanbul, the central authorities did not uproot the local gentry, whose fortified houses in some parts of the area continued to dominate the countryside. On the contrary, these people were incorporated into the sub-provincial administration, particularly where the protection of the Damascus pilgrimage caravan to Mecca was concerned. Only in the 1630s, after serious local uprisings had been suppressed, was there an attempt to eliminate these grandees from the provincial administration.[5] Centralization thus came rather late in the day.

Central Rule Mediated through Provincial Notables

If in the province of Damascus and its neighbors, Ottoman ambitions to rule directly were rather short-lived, this tendency towards decentralization was part of an empire-wide trend. From the 17th century onwards governors increasingly were expected to finance their own military forces, and this meant either farming local taxes or else cooperating with established tax farmers. After 1695 it became possible to acquire tax farms on a lifetime basis, and whoever held such major farms had a good chance of governing the province, even if his official title was more modest. Often the governor was in office only for a short period or for the most part absent on campaigns, so that real power was exercised by the receivers of taxes that he appointed. In addition, recruiting the armed bands that a governor was expected to bring to the sultans' campaigns cost money; and this money had to be raised by the people who had the bad luck to live in the relevant province. Such demands were typically for lump sums; and distributing the total levy over villages and taxpayers might be a source of power. By demanding less from one village and making its neighbors make up the deficit, a small-scale tax collector could acquire clients and thereby develop a local power base.

In areas that were visited by foreign merchants, such notables could moreover expand their power base by selling the goods that they had collected as taxes. Or else notables used their contacts with foreign merchants to mediate business deals for the peasants: while the mediators profited in terms of money and social power, the sellers, at least in some cases, got better prices than they would have received on their own. Such commercial arrangements meant that an intermediate stratum imposed itself between the government in Istanbul and the provincial population.

Some notables of this type were able to increase their power to the point of becoming magnates, who in the 18th and 19th centuries came to govern their territories with very limited interference from Istanbul. When, however, the central administration considered such a personage to have become a major threat, it was common practice to entice his rivals in the same or neighboring provinces to attack him. The victim then was deposed, executed, and his possessions confiscated; soon after, these items were sold to claimants for the vacant position that might include members of the dead man's family. As a result, in some provinces there emerged dynasties that held on to power for a couple of decades.

Particularly in the Arab provinces, these families or "politically active households," established by military men, might demonstrate their ascendancy by sumptuous public construction. Mosques were part of this program, and Mosul and Baghdad benefited from the attempts of local rulers to redistribute wealth and leave their imprint on the cityscape; in some regions new combinations of charitable endowments were created. These developments have greatly interested art historians, who currently show considerable interest in the findings of "regular" Ottoman historians. Palaces also might assert the power of the local dynasty, as happened in Damascus but also, and quite dramatically, in the eastern Anatolian town of Doğu Beyazit, close to the Iranian border.

In spite of their obvious power, the number of magnates aspiring to independent royalty remained quite limited. It has been suggested that lifetime tax farms contributed substantially toward securing their loyalty to the sultan; for these revenue sources surely would be jeopardized once the Ottoman Empire was no longer available to legitimize the extraction of taxes.[6] Furthermore in many cases there were several lifetime tax farmers who claimed revenue from the same region. If one of the competitors were to set up a petty principality, the others were likely to lose their claims; and this situation explains why the central government found it so easy to mobilize magnates or notables against one another.

Decentralization or power-sharing with local notables thus probably had a stabilizing function in the 18th-century Ottoman Empire, as these power brokers were kept in dependence to the sultan. While once widespread, claims that these developments necessarily represented a "decline" are today viewed with skepticism. After all, while decentralization began in the late 16th century, the Ottoman Empire held together reasonably well for about two hundred years more, not a bad performance as empires go. In the same vein, scholars today do not consider these assorted magnates to be proto-nationalists, as was common among historians of the Arab world some forty years ago. Ethnically, these provincial power-brokers usually had nothing in common with the populations that they taxed and controlled; and in those cases in which we can make out a cultural orientation, these personages identified themselves as Ottoman gentlemen and not as representatives of local populations. Whether they negotiated on behalf of the latter, securing tax and other benefits, and thus acted as a kind of informal representative, or alternatively exploited the tax-payers of their province without giving much in return, depended on circumstance; it is impossible to give a universally valid answer to this question.

Peace, Foreign Trade,
and the Capitulations

Economic historians have long since concluded that the Ottoman Empire possessed a reasonably strong commercial base, largely due to the size of the domestic market. Moreover, caravan routes to Asia continued to be important well into the early 1800s, and were not marginalized by oceanic trade in the 17th century as had long been assumed. Throughout the 16th and 17th centuries, merchants subject to the sultans, both Muslim and non-Muslim, traded with Iran and India to the east and Venice, Holland, England, and France to the west. Venice was a magnet, being the only Christian city routinely vis-ited by Muslim traders. By the 1700s the Habsburg domains also gained importance as trading partners; this area was mainly fre-quented by Orthodox merchants who sold yarn to textile manufac-turers and leather to saddlers and shoemakers. Even the Leipzig fairs were frequented by sizeable numbers of Ottoman subjects. Thus offi-cial emphasis on the expansion of the realm of Islam did not imply that peaceful relations with "unbelievers" were considered impossible

or that Ottoman Muslims were officially discouraged from trading
with outsiders to the realm.

In this domain as in so many others, pragmatism was dominant:
Mehmed the Conqueror (r. 1451-81), for instance, hoped to reroute
the international spice trade through Istanbul, his newly conquered
capital, an enterprise for which he would have needed the cooperation
of Venetian, Genoese, and other foreign traders from non-Muslim
countries. In the late 16th and early 17th centuries as well, the
Ottoman administration was very conscious of the fact that protecting traders meant that the exchequer would benefit from customs revenues. When discussing this issue with foreign rulers like the hereditary princes of Mecca, known as the Sharifs, but also with the Doge
of Venice, the officials of the sultan liked to point out that if a rulei
did not protect traders, they would stop coming, and that could only
be harmful to princely finances. Privileges to Muslims at the expense
of non-Muslim competitors were not at issue in these exchanges.

Trade could be properly conducted only in times of peace; when
the sultan was at war with a given ruler, his/her subjects normally left
the realm, although commerce was often continued through local
intermediaries, or else through neutrals. Revenue aside, the support of
trade might yield political benefits; and as the sultans' servitors often
viewed commerce in this light, they were willing to provide privileges
to the subjects of foreign potentates – known in European parlance
as capitulations.[7] These grants allowed traders and other sojourners
subject to a given ruler, who was the actual grantee, a degree of
immunity from Ottoman taxation and administrative rulings.
Sovereigns whose subjects benefited in this manner were not necessarily part of Christendom. In the 16th century as in the 18th,
Armenian merchants subject to the Shah of Iran, known as the Acem
tüccarı, enjoyed similar privileges, and when they wished to submit
complaints to the sultan's administration, they did so through the
mediation of their consul, called the *şehbender.*

The Challenges of French and British Traders

While in the 16th and 17th centuries capitulations in Ottoman law were regarded as unilateral grants of the sultans that these rulers could abrogate at will, by the later 1700s these concessions were to turn into serious limitations of Ottoman sovereignty. From a long-term perspective, this change was connected to the defeats of the 1680s and 1690s, when for the first time the sultans made political concessions to Louis XIV of France in return for diplomatic support against the Habsburgs.

Special exemptions from Ottoman administrative interventions were granted not only to ambassadors and consuls, but also to their servitors, including the interpreters through whom the sultans' government needed to be approached. One of the major abuses of capitulations-based privilege was due to this convention, namely the issuing of certificates as "interpreters" to non-Muslim merchants in large numbers. Often these people did not even reside in the towns where they were supposedly employed or were ignorant of the relevant languages. European consuls and ambassadors, while often recognizing that the practice was a serious abuse, employed these pseudo-interpreters because a large crowd of clients raised the prestige of the diplomat in question; in many cases, moreover, the interpreter candidates paid good money for the privilege of being employed. From the non-Muslim merchants' perspective—as we have come to appreciate in recent years—the investment made sense, especially in the second half of the 18th century, when the pressing needs of the exchequer sometimes resulted in confiscations on flimsy pretexts or even without any legally acceptable reason. People who could claim the protection of a foreign state typically were immune from such exactions.

Seeking the protection of foreign embassies or consuls was not a strategy open to Muslim merchants; the privileged position of Christian and Jewish protégés, who in time might even become subjects of the state protecting them, must therefore have given rise to many complaints about unfair treatment. While Selim III (r. 1789-1807) and Mahmud II (r. 1808-39) issued privileges to woo both

Muslim and non-Muslim merchants away from foreign protection, the numbers of people so favored were quite limited. Moreover, for some traders and artisans, enjoying "foreign protection" was more than just a business advantage: it became part of their self-image.[8] Thus the entire issue should be regarded as part and parcel of the crisis that the Empire suffered in the late 18th century.

Confronting the Tsars

While the Ottoman socio-political system worked reasonably well until the 1760s, after that difficulties came thick and fast. War was the major problem. A recent work has stressed the military disadvantages of the long period of relative peace between 1718 and 1768. For as a result, the changes in the conduct of battle that took place in Europe during the War of the Austrian Succession and the Seven Years' War were not incorporated by the Ottomans until it was already too late. However, this relative withdrawal from armed confrontation is but one aspect of a more complex problem: for the Empire desperately needed peace in order to recuperate from the destructive wars of 1683-1718; and the relative peacefulness of the mid-18th century had even made a moderate expansion of manufacturing possible. Yet without some economic growth, there is no telling whether the Empire would have held up during the crises that followed; Ottoman policy-makers were thus caught between the devil and the deep blue sea.

Even more seriously perhaps, the Russian Empire was much better endowed with all the resources needed for warfare than the Ottomans. Enormous forests provided wood for shipbuilding in much larger quantities than were available in the semi-arid zones where the sultans' territories were mostly situated. Metals were also quite abundant, and after the peasants subject to the tsars had expanded southward into the fertile "black earth" lands, grain was also cultivated in significant quantities. Once these resources could be mobilized, due to the political rearrangements enforced by emperors/empresses such as Peter I (1672-1725) and Catherine II (1729-96), it became very difficult for the Ottomans to regain the initiative. Still, recent research has also stressed the fact that Russian serf-soldiers were poorly fed and supplied in comparison to their Ottoman counterparts, although as a result, the baggage trains supplying the sultans' armies during 18th-century campaigns were large and costly.[9]

These competitive disadvantages were probably understood in Istanbul only at a late date because the early efforts of Tsar Peter to build up a navy had not been very successful, nor had been his military campaigns against the Ottomans on land. The entrance of a Russian naval squadron into the Mediterranean was thus quite unprecedented, and so was the virtual annihilation of the Ottoman fleet near Çeşme in 1770. Moreover, between the Treaty of Küçük Kaynarca in 1774 and outright Russian annexation nine years later, the Crimea was lost to the Ottoman Empire, an event all the more traumatic as now a Muslim population was involved. These losses must have led to a legitimization crisis as well; but remarkably enough, none of the sultans lost his throne because of the defeats of the 1770s and 1780s.

Throughout the 19th century the Russian tsars remained the Ottomans' principal opponents. Much of the fighting for territory took place in Moldavia and Walachia, in today's terms Moldova and Rumania, respectively. Once Serbs and Bulgarians had gained a degree of local autonomy, the tsars patronized these polities. Many political figures in the Russian Empire hoped for an ultimate partition of Ottoman territory in which they would gain Istanbul; these projects were first formulated by Catherine II, who named one of her grandsons Constantine in anticipation.

Reshaping the Empire: New Perspectives
on the Reforms of the 19th Century

Given the bitter experience of the wars against Russia, Selim III attempted to replace the janissaries, whose military value by now was highly questionable, with troops trained according to a "new model"

(*Nizam cedid*). The attempt misfired: the sultan was deposed and ultimately killed. New studies of the sultan's policies and their ramifications are currently underway; one of them concerns the attitude of the Ottoman notables as a group during those crisis years, and another investigates the actual rebellion that brought down Sultan Selim in 1807. In addition, there are two projects that focus on the Tatar khanate, with considerable emphasis on its later years, whose results will hopefully be published soon. As we can therefore expect a rather extensive re-thinking of our previous assumptions, which to a considerable degree are based on studies undertaken thirty or forty years ago, it is only prudent to avoid any sweeping claims.

Much work is also being done on the Tanzimat, the major administrative refashioning that in the middle of the 19th century was supposed to make the Empire competitive in a rapidly changing world, where ever more sophisticated technologies were available to European governments and wars could no longer be won without them. While older studies have generally dwelt on the inefficiency of the old structures and their relative imperviousness to reform from above, our perspectives have changed quite dramatically during the last few years.[10] In the context of "multiple modernities," historians have concluded that the route to modernization as followed by England and France was not the only one possible. Japan, imperial Russia, and China all undertook significant socio-political measures that can be described as "modernization." The Ottoman Empire also launched its own variety: beginning with the restructuring of the military, sultans and viziers then proceeded to revamp the bureaucracy, the legal framework within which the administrative apparatus was expected to function, and last but not least, education.[11]

As refashioning the military so as to make it once again capable of winning wars was the major motivating factor, many of the newer studies focus on this issue. The plans of Sultan Mahmud II and the grand viziers of the mid-1800s were inspired by the example of Mehmed Ali/Muhammad Ali Pasha, governor and later viceroy of Egypt. The latter had built an army that not only reconquered the holy cities of Mecca and Medina for the sultan, but when it came to armed conflict with the sultan, also defeated whatever forces Mahmud II could mobilize against him. Recent research has made us aware of the tremendous sacrifices that this policy demanded from the population of Egypt.

In conformity with the model instituted by its rebellious governor, the Ottoman central administration began the search for recruits that were to serve in the army for long years and, after having gone through the relevant drills, fight battles in the European style. Non-Muslims were considered undesirable except in certain technical capacities, and the recruitment of Muslim Turks was disproportionate; apparently it was heavy enough to result in a lower-than-average rate of population growth. By contrast, certain Albanian clans that in previous generations had served as irregulars in the Ottoman army in exchange for tax exemptions were now given to understand that their services were no longer required and that they would have to provide taxes and recruits like everyone else. Refusal to conform was deemed a sign of "savageness" and merited serious coercion. It might thus happen that while trying to cement loyalties, the late Ottoman state created disaffection where none had existed before.[12]

Revamping the bureaucracy and establishing a police service presented further challenges. These enterprises were also part of the state formation project, which is how today's historians interpret the Tanzimat. Historians now highlight the concrete activities of officials "in the field," for instance the activities of reforming governors such as Midhat Paşa (1822-83). Reform meant that the literary skills that had previously characterized an accomplished scribe were no longer much in demand. To speak with Carter Findley, post-Tanzimat officials no longer saw themselves as craftsmen producing correctly worded and calligraphically exquisite documents, but as people committed to implementing particular policies.[13]

Studies of bureaucratic reform include internal matters such as recruitment, hierarchical structures, promotion patterns, and sociability. Formal training of future administrators in a special school known as the Mülkiye was instituted, and examinations began to play a role in determining the placement of officials. Ministries were formed and recruited specialized personnel: in the mid-19th century one of the main routes to high office was service in the translation chamber, where young officials learned French and diplomatic skills, which they honed while serving as junior secretaries in the Ottoman embassy in Paris. But at the same time, it remained possible to make a successful bureaucratic career by establishing old-style patronage relations, sometimes cemented by membership in a dervish order. The government's lack of money was a major impediment to reform: with salaries low and frequently in arrears, it was impossible for many officials to subsist if they did not take fees that might shade off into bribes. Urban policemen often were caught between the conflicting expectations of their superiors and the townspeople they were supposed to control; due to the combination of low pay and exposure to socio-political pressures, this service found it especially difficult to attract literate and well-informed persons.[14] As access to the personnel files of the Hamidian period has now become possible, it seems that studies of the police apparatus are on the verge of "taking off."[15]

The new bureaucracy operated according to new laws, often adapted from European models. What adaptations were deemed necessary and how the changes were received by different sectors of the population is currently a topic of study. In addition, scholars concern themselves with the spread of private property, especially but not exclusively land. Projects of this kind have become possible because of the grand series of registers through which, in the 1840s, the government attempted to gain an overview of the taxable resources of its realm. They are now available to investigators, although it will take time before we can properly understand the considerations that prompted officials to selectively record information and taxpayers to provide the necessary data, doubtless also on a selective basis. However, it already has become clear that at least in the more accessible and commercialized districts, for instance on the Aegean coast of Anatolia, the difficulties involved in such data collection were not fundamentally different from those experienced by people in charge of comparable projects in the more remote provinces of France.

Information gathering was a crucial part of early 19th-century modernization. Some of these projects were connected with repression: in the early 1800s attempts were made to survey the population of Istanbul house by house, so as to weed out the jobless and those whose occupations were officially were deemed "unnecessary," and send them back to their provinces of origin. Apparently Sultan Selim III aimed to reduce the number of mouths to feed in the capital and perhaps also get rid of people who might take to the streets in support of janissary claims. These surveys, unparalleled in earlier times, are now being studied by urban historians.[16] In the 1830s an attempt was made to count the male population in many provinces of the Empire, in order to locate men who might be drafted into the army. Not surprisingly, this aim became widely known, and many potential draftees fled. Moreover, in the 1840s the government employed a large number of well-paid informers to report what was being said about matters of public concern, both in public and in private. Unlike in later cases of this type, the people thus reported were not to be punished; the aim was merely to survey "public opinion."[17] These projects all indicate that governments of the day were conscious of the value of information. During the last few years historians have shown that within the limits of available technology, pre-Tanzimat governments were in the business of data collection.

As we have seen, bureaucrats in the new ministries, as well as military officers, had to be educated in schools, and here the strategy adopted by the Ottoman elite rather resembled the practices found in many European countries. Arrangements were made for professional education while the preparation of the students for these programs was usually insufficient; professional schools therefore tended to institute their own preparatory courses. A sequence of schools from which students needed to graduate before they could tackle the next stage was instituted quite late; and at the lower levels, skills and information quite often took second place to the inculcation of piety and loyalty to the sultan. Given the small number of civilian high schools, certain Muslim families sent their children to missionary schools in spite of repeated official prohibitions. At the level of higher education too, civilian professions remained a poor relation to the technical expertise that could be acquired in the military; the University of Istanbul only began to function regularly in 1900. As a result non-Muslims and latter also Muslims who could afford it quite often arranged for their sons to study abroad. Given this state of affairs, a good general education was a major piece of "cultural capital;" and when in the early 20th century quite a few younger members of the elite concluded that the Ottoman Empire was unlikely to last much longer, they often used their educations to make careers for themselves in newly developing branches such as university teaching, communications, publishing, and entertainment.

The Last Decades of the Ottoman Empire in Current Historiography

In Ottoman studies, the years from 1840 to 1922 are currently being investigated with great intensity; this is due at least in part to the enormous mass of documentation that has recently become available. The archives in Istanbul are now accessible for the Hamidian period, including the documentation originally stored in the Yıldız palace, from which sultan Abdülhamid II (r. 1876-1909) ran his government. These archives have yielded material for a number of semi-official document publications.

Political considerations play a major role as well. Among the Turkish public there is an enormous demand for the commemoration of the battle of Çanakkale/Gallipoli (1915), a concern shared in certain circles in Britain, Australia, and New Zealand as well. For a non-specialist, it is often impossible to say where historical research ends; and the cultivation of memory takes over. Viewed from a broader perspective, the emergence of nationalism in the Balkans and afterwards in Syria and in the Turkish provinces, the Armenian disaster, the history of Muslim refugees from the Balkans and the Caucasus, and the fates of the victims of the Greco-Turkish population exchange have all motivated scholars to delve into the archives. Some of them write in order to defend a political position; attempts at a more or less detached survey of actions and attitudes are few and far between. At present, a consensus is nowhere in sight.

In the long run work in the Russian archives will probably change our perceptions of the "great game" between the British and Russian governments in various regions of Asia, including certain Ottoman territories, just as research in the Japanese archives has allowed a more realistic evaluation of Meiji policies towards the Ottomans than had been possible from published sources alone. For the present, imperialism and the "Eastern Question" have mainly been studied on the basis of British archives and materials from western and central Europe. The accessibility of the Public Record Office in London must have motivated many historians to focus on the materials found there. Yet other factors play a role as well: while imperialism has a strong economic dimension, the Ottoman archives apparently do not contain a lot of material from which statistics relevant to production, investment, and trade can be compiled. Also located in Istanbul, the archives of the Banque Ottomane, a foreign-owned bank that played a central role in the financial dependence of the last Ottoman decades, have now been catalogued and studied by a few researchers; but they remain difficult to access.

As for monographs, as we have already seen, considerable work has been done on the bureaucracy and the educational system. Documents in the central archives are helpful because they reflect Ottoman attitudes in negotiations with foreign powers and companies. This emphasis probably explains why in the last few years we have seen a crop of new studies on railway construction, an issue that acquires a new dimension when Ottoman concerns can be taken into account. Institutions and cultural history are also being brought to the fore: the city administrations, founded for the most part during the last quarter of the 19th century, are a favorite topic, especially since in recent years, municipalities have been active in promoting a sense that "our town is our home." Istanbul has attracted the most attention, but we also have detailed work on Salonika and certain towns in Syria and Palestine, as well as North Africa. These monographs are especially interesting because in city administrations, career bureaucrats

almost always needed to work together with ad hoc committees of
local notables who, given the notorious lack of money in the state's
coffers, provided the financing for certain projects. Accordingly, they
also demanded to be heard when it came to establishing priorities;
and in many places these personages might themselves take the initiative when it came to public works. As a corollary, the emerging
beaux quartiers of many Ottoman towns were notoriously better supplied with even basic utilities than the poorer parts, a problem that
continues to the present day in certain places. Work on urban renewal, post-Tanzimat style, thus implies studying the interface of officialdom and at least the upper levels of urban society.[18]

As for the laboring classes and their places of work, studies of factories have been undertaken by historians working in Bulgaria; for it
was here that proto-industrial weaving of woolen cloth was first
moved into factories when dependable orders came in from the reorganized Ottoman army. However, other factories that produced partly for state needs and partly for the market were soon established in
and around Istanbul, and some of the documents produced in these
institutions have recently become accessible. From these sources it has
emerged that only some of the workers were hired on the "regular"
labor market; others were boys serving in the factories after they had
been sentenced to reform school. Yet others were young non-Muslims
who in the 19th century were not being drafted into the army, but
instead were sometimes called up to do their military service in state
factories.[19] Draftees also played a major role in the coal mines of
Zonguldak in northern Anatolia: some were villagers who, in the
manner that had been customary since the 16th century, were made
to spend a number of months every year servicing the mines and
extracting minerals. Others were workmen who had been transformed
into soldiers during wartime. All these people suffered badly from
accidents and diseases that often could have been avoided through
more investment and better education.[20]

But most Ottoman industrial production took place not in factories or mines but in small enterprises: for it has been shown that the
ever-increasing importation of foreign products after 1815 did not

result in the disappearance of local manufacturers. The latter often remained in business by self-exploitation and the exploitation of apprentices and family members, practices which have been well described by the term "labor squeezing."[21] In order to stay competitive, such enterprises typically sold their products at prices that made capital accumulation and investment all but impossible. These observations and interpretations are highly important; but even so, the history of Ottoman workers is still in its beginnings.

In terms of cultural history, we can study the changing face of Ottoman towns and cities, because in the second half of the 19th century a growing number of people developed an interest in drawing or painting cityscapes. Even more dramatic was the increasing interest in photography; and there survive large accumulations of official and unofficial photos showing the larger cities of the Empire and "tourist centers" such as Jerusalem. Photographs of people at their workplaces in schools, hospitals, construction sites, and factories also survive in substantial numbers. Of course, photographs need to be studied just as critically as written sources: thus it has emerged that as foreign tourists demanded certain kinds of pictures as souvenirs, studios often made them up. "Picturesque" street artisans or languid Ottoman ladies thus might be impersonated by people whom the photographers could mobilize for that purpose. In a different vein, recent studies have taught us that the photo albums which Sultan Abdülhamid sent to foreign governments were intended to convey a political message: the Ottoman Empire was now possessed of all the accoutrements of modernity. Therefore, by implication, there was no reason for any outsiders to intervene in the process of Ottoman modernization. Whether this discourse was appreciated at the receiving end is yet a different topic of study. Photographs thus imply statements, and it is the historian's job to tease out what their authors wanted to say.

Printing, publishing, and the book trade in Istanbul and the Empire's major cities have attracted interest for a long time already, and the same can be said of the theater. However, recent studies concern more specific issues such as the role of women in communications: a specialized institution known as the Kadın Eserleri Kütüphanesi (Library of Women's Works) attempts to bring together all works written and published by Ottoman and Turkish women, and its collections provide a starting point for research in this field. Another recent interest is censorship, a practice that emerged together with the new means of communication in the mid-19th century.[22] Newspapers and periodicals were affected, but most dramatic was the physical destruction of a prominent literary theater whose plays had displeased Sultan Abdülhamid. When the latter's absolutism was at its height, it therefore became virtually impossible to bring out original theatrical works in Turkish.

For the period after the fall of Sultan Abdülhamid, when the Committee of Union and Progress (Ittihad ve terakki) first impacted the government "from without" and after 1913 directly ruled the Empire, sources in the Ottoman archives are accessible only to a limited extent. Researchers therefore rely on foreign archives and libraries, or else on published material, which is of interest especially for the months immediately following the revolution of 1908, when for a short time, censorship was abolished. We possess significant monographs on the ideology of the Committee members and on their behavior while in opposition. A recent study has attempted to show that Sultan Abdülhamid was forced to turn himself into a constitutional monarch not merely by a military coup d'état, as had previously been assumed, but by tax strikes and other manifestations of public discontent that were serious enough to be called an authentic revolution. Other work concerns the increasing incorporation of women into the labor force due to the loss of male workers during World War I: here the government took a hand to remedy, at least minimally, the appalling poverty of soldiers' wives.[23]

Work has also been done on the war economy. In the years preceding the First World War, the losses of territory in the Balkans and elsewhere had sparked powerful nationalist reactions among the Turkish population. As a result, the political elites came to the conclusion that they could no longer trust non-Muslim businessmen and should try to create a Muslim bourgeoisie through state aid. But as "regular" accumulation through commerce, agriculture, and industry seemed too slow, there was a strong inclination to confiscate and redistribute property. As for the "battle against speculation and hoarding" during World War I, while largely ineffective as far as consumers were concerned, it provided plenty of opportunities to impose harsh penalties upon non-Muslim businessmen – a classical case of "primitive accumulation" in the Marxian sense; petty Muslim traders suffered as well. Moreover, the war fought in Anatolia and the Armenian deportation provided further occasion for confiscation. The resources thus made available were redistributed to favored businessmen. As the principal specialist on the Committee's war financing has concluded, adherents of "Union and Progress" stood a good chance of making their fortunes, while those without such affiliation were likely to lose out.[24]

Ottomans and Japanese in a World Dominated by Imperialism

How did all this compare to the experience of other modernizing countries outside of North America and western and central Europe? As we have seen, Ottoman restructuring was undertaken in order to secure the continued existence of the Empire, and throughout the world there were other polities in a comparable situation. Japan was a prime example of such defensive modernization that greatly impressed the Ottoman reading public of the late 19th and early 20th centuries. It is therefore rather interesting to review the comparative research that has been undertaken on this issue.

Without major structural changes, once Admiral Perry's American ships had enforced the opening of Japanese ports and unequal treaties had been concluded with Western powers, the danger of becoming yet another European/American colony was clear to the political elite in Tokyo. Getting rid of these treaties as soon as feasible therefore became a major aim. Furthermore, by the late 1800s asserting Great Power status by concluding unequal treaties of their own became part of the Japanese elite's agenda where the Ottomans were concerned. Profuse expressions of friendship and reference to a common "Asian background" notwithstanding, the Japanese tended to view the late Ottoman Empire as a polity akin to Qing/Manchu China, which in 1895 had been forced to sign an unequal treaty with Japan. However, in spite of their political weakness, the successive governments of the sultans were able to rebuff this demand, and diplomatic relations were established only with the Republic of Turkey in 1924, when unequal treaties no longer were part of the agenda.[25]

Japanese society began its modernization process with significant advantages that included widespread literacy even in rural areas, agriculture open to commercially oriented modernization, a high level of urbanization, and an upper class of former military men who were able and willing to re-launch themselves as entrepreneurs. In the educational sector, Japan's head start was particularly striking: in 1868, when the Japanese population totaled 35 million, male literacy stood at 40 percent and total literacy at twenty; as a result, the Japanese elite had a much easier time convincing the dominant male section of the population of the need for profound change. Moreover, the Meiji reforms rapidly raised literacy rates for the population as a whole: in 1923 the Japanese rate already stood at close to 80 percent.

As for the Ottoman route to modernity, it is worth discussing the differences from the Japanese experience. Literacy and secular education were limited to relatively small groups, mainly connected to the armed forces. Moreover, late Ottoman campaigns to teach the three basic skills of reading, writing, and arithmetic were of limited impact: in 1923, when the Turkish Republic was founded, the total literacy rate was about 15 percent of a population of 15 million. To further complicate matters, while in Japan most centers of population and trade were easily accessible by sea, the long overland routes of the Ottoman domain made communications costly and difficult. Commercial agriculture therefore was viable only in certain areas.

Cities in late Tokugawa Japan thrived commercially. What is more, the capital generated in them was locally owned: after all, the long isolation and political pacification of the country since the early 17th century had been propitious to the accumulation of capital. By contrast, in the Ottoman realm, the political setup had made the accumulation of productive capital in the hands of tax-paying subjects relatively difficult even in the 16th century, to say nothing of less prosperous times. Moreover, the many wars of the 18th and 19th centuries had resulted in the loss of much productive capacity previously established in the Balkans; and the onerous conditions under which the mid-19th-century Ottoman government borrowed money from European lenders to finance the modernization of army and communications further contributed to budgetary deficits. By 1875 bankruptcy was the result; and due to financial tutelage by a consortium of European lenders, the governments of Abdülhamid and the Young Turks had only limited access to the taxes collected in their territory. None of this had happened in Japan.

A further complication arose from the fact that by the mid-19th century much of the accumulated capital available in the Ottoman realm belonged to non-Muslim merchants, who increasingly were caught up in the nationalist currents of the times. No parallel to this situation existed in Japan, where non-Japanese groups lived on the margins, both socially and territorially; they certainly had no access to "foreign protection" and were not prime accumulators of capital. Given these major differences, the expectation that the Ottomans should have been able to duplicate the Japanese performance hardly seems realistic.

Recent Attempts at Synthesis and Inter-Field Collaboration

In the 1960s, 1970s, and early 1980s many Ottoman historians felt that the right time for synthesis had not yet arrived. In my view at the time this hesitation made sense, for archival work tended to focus on limited questions, and it was often far from clear what conclusions should be drawn from the research. Apart from the efforts of Ismail Hakkı Uzunçarşılı, in this period only Halil Inalcik and the couple Stanford and Ezel K. Shaw attempted to provide overviews over long time spans. It soon became clear that specialization by period and/or subject was becoming widespread in the Ottomanist field as elsewhere, and collaboration thus became a prime necessity.[26] While a scholar such as Fuat Köprülü (1890-1966) had combined work on Ottoman literature and history, to later generations these two fields had become quite distinct and could only be adequately treated by a dialog between specialists. In response to this situation, in the late 1980s and in the course of the 1990s several collaborative works were published in France, Turkey, and England.[27] While these works were intended for advanced students and researchers, Justin McCarthy courageously attempted a one-volume presentation, notable for its emphasis on environmental factors.[28]

However, with the "opening up" of Ottoman history to the wider world during the last ten years or so, we observe what may be described as a two-pronged development. On the one hand, syntheses both by groups of scholars and by individuals continue to appear: presently in course of publication is the four-volume *Cambridge History of Turkey* that in reality encompasses mainly the Ottoman Empire. Given the centrality of warfare to the life of early modern states, the monumental work by Virginia Aksan on Ottoman wars is an investigation into the state structures that mobilized the subjects' resources, fed the ever-expanding soldiery, and recruited military men; this work can just as well be read as a history of Ottoman state-society relations in the 1700s and 1800s. In addition, there is the massive yet highly readable one-volume history by Caroline Finkel, a unique example of a best-selling work based on an intimate knowledge particularly of Ottoman chronicles.[29]

The second route of communication between Ottoman historians and their colleagues in neighboring fields consists of collaborative work documented in edited volumes. Typically, a historian of the Roman world, China, or most frequently early modern Europe will organize a project on some broad and encompassing theme: my own experience in this sector includes collaborative studies of artisans' migrations, cotton production, narratives written in the first person, festivities, periodization in history, eighteenth-century urban culture, and others, to say nothing of the recently popular projects to study the operation of empires. While in the past Ottoman historians were rarely invited to participate in such ventures, this tendency is now changing, even though perhaps an invitation extended to a "token Ottomanist" can be viewed as the proverbial swallow that does not mean the beginning of summer. However, the scarcity of funding for the humanities and social sciences in many European countries has induced quite a few historians concerned with this region to network outside of their own fields, and practitioners of Ottoman history have benefited as a consequence.

To Conclude

After a lengthy stay in a kind of limbo where a few specialists concentrated on more or less arcane research, Ottoman history during the last ten to fifteen years has been gathering pace and coming out into the open. New sources have been made available not only in the archives but also in libraries. While until the 1990s most narrative sources were accessible only in manuscripts or else in unsatisfactory editions usually dating from the 19th century, many Ottoman chronicles and embassy reports are now available in critical editions, or at least in renditions of the texts accompanied by introductions providing some information on the author and the conditions under which he wrote his work. As an example, we may mention the ten-volume edition of the travelogue of the 17th-century writer Evliya Çelebi, without whose account writing the social history of that period of Ottoman history would be very difficult indeed: after twelve years as a work in progress, the edition is now complete, as the tenth and final volume appeared at the end of 2007.[30]

Certainly the level of sophistication with which we treat our sources often still leaves much to be desired. As this rapid overview has shown, the gaps in our research are numerous; and many works that we write today will presumably make our successors smile as they are found to be impossibly naïve. But it is exciting to see that our discipline is going somewhere – may the good work continue . . .

CHAPTER 1

◆ ◆ ◆

Rise and Expansion
(1299-1481)

The Beginnings of the Ottoman Polity

The oldest information concerning an Ottoman small principality takes us back to the first quarter of the 14th century. At first this was only one of the numerous small polities that filled the power vacuum that had arisen when the empire of the Anatolian Seljuks had dissolved in the second half of the 13th century and the Mongolian sovereigns in Iran were retreating from their Anatolian possessions in the first half of the 14th century. The most important competitors of the expanding Ottomans included the princes of Eretna, whose center was in Sivas, and the far longer-lived central Anatolian polity founded by the Karaman dynasty. The Aydın and Menteşe families who ruled in southwest Anatolia were also serious competitors, at least for a time.

The chronological succession of the first Ottoman conquests is not easy to determine. The early Ottoman chronicles, most of which were written towards the end of the 15th century, long after the events in question, are generally vague on chronology. Late medieval accounts penned in the various principalities of the Balkan Peninsula were not much better on this score. For this reason, today's standard works contain a variety of dates even for some key events, such as the conquest of Edirne. The first very important city the Ottomans seized under their founding sultan, Osman I (1299-1326), was Bursa. Iznik, which in the mid-thirteenth century had been home to Byzantine rulers in exile, followed in 1337. Until the conquest of Edirne (circa 1361), Bursa remained the Ottoman capital. But even when the sultans were living in Edirne for the most part, they continued to build their imposing mosques in Bursa (where they are still preserved) until the conquest of Constantinople/Istanbul in 1453. When an earthquake destroyed the walls of the city of Gelibolu in 1352, Sultan Orhan (1326-1362) was able to enter the city easily and conquer his first important harbor site.

In 1355, the death of Stefan Dušan initiated the decline of the Serbian Empire. From 1363-1365, a series of Ottoman military campaigns in Thrace and present-day southern Bulgaria culminated in the conquest of Plovdiv (earlier: Philippopolis, Filibe). One of the last Crusades was organized by French, Burgundian, Hungarian, and other European rulers to support Constantinople, besieged by Bayezid I (1389-1402). This Crusade, whose commanders also had more far-reaching ambitions, ended with the utter defeat of the European knights (Nicopolis/Niğbolu, 1396). The result was a consolidation of the Ottoman conquests in Europe. Although the invasion of Timur (often written in the Latinized form Tamerlane, from Timur Lenk, "Timur the Lame") led to the complete, albeit temporary, collapse of Ottoman rule in Asia Minor, none of the Balkan princes were able to cast off Ottoman rule over his former territory permanently during these years, when the sons of the deposed Bayezid were competing for the throne.

Timur did not remain in Anatolia for long. After the 1403 conquest of Izmir, which was still controlled by Crusaders, he returned to Central Asia, where he died in 1405. After a long Interregnum, Mehmed I was established as the Ottoman sole ruler (1413-1421). But there was further expansion as early as the 1420s, beginning in Anatolia. In 1425, Izmir and the southwestern principalities of Teke and Menteşe were reconquered. Salonika, long the second-largest city in the Byzantine Empire, followed in 1430. In 1439 the Serbian state ceased to exist. At that time the Kingdom of Hungary, which had occupied the fortress city of Belgrade for quite some time, was the major adversary of the Ottomans in southeastern Europe.

The Age of Mehmed the Conqueror

Under these circumstances the Byzantine "empire" was little more than an enclave in Ottoman territory. Only Constantinople remained after several failed sieges (there was a blockade from 1394 on) because its strong walls and location were conducive to an effective defense. But when the young sultan Mehmed II ascended to the Ottoman throne in 1451, he immediately began building the fortress of Rumelihisarı, still extant today, to prevent the passage of enemy ships through the Bosporus. He also used artillery to bombard the walls of Constantinople, which had not been reinforced to withstand it. After a brief siege, the city fell into Ottoman hands in May 1453.

All in all, the reign of Mehmed II was a time of rapid Ottoman expansion. In the North, the principality of the Crimean Tatars, one of the remnants of Mongolian rule in what is Russia and the Ukraine today, became a dependent principality in 1475. The Genoese colonies on the Black Sea were at first tributary to the sultan, and outright military conquest soon followed; the Genoese colony of Caffa became the Ottoman provincial capital of Kefe. The small principality ruled by the Komnenos dynasty, which claimed the title of Empire of Trebizond, was conquered in 1461 and soon Islamicized by means of resettlement and conversion of local people. In Anatolia, the Karamanoğulları principality was defeated and incorporated into the Ottoman state between 1469 and 1474. As a result, the Ottomans expanded into central Anatolia and Mehmed the Conqueror's empire now bordered on the territories that had long been subordinate to the Mamluk sultanate of Syria and Egypt.

In southeastern Europe, the Peloponnesus was conquered from the Franks and Byzantines and henceforth became the Ottoman province of Mora (1460-1464). Venice also suffered serious losses (Euboa/Negroponte became Ottoman in 1470) after the Ottoman vanguard of Mehmed II reached the easternmost part of northern Italy in 1478. Mehmed II had a fortress built in Elbasan, Albania; after the death of the Albanian Prince George Kastriota/Skanderbeg in 1468, all of Albania was under the firm control of the Ottomans. Groups of

Albanians who could not come to terms with this state of affairs migrated to southern Italy. But in 1480 the Italian fortress town of namely Otranto was also conquered by an Ottoman military contingent. This event was probably intended as a first step toward the conquest of Italy, but when Mehmed II died the following year, his son Bayezid II (1481-1512) set different priorities, and the Ottomans retreated from Otranto.

At the Border

The Ottoman state was situated at the edge of the Islamic world, and could thus command resources not available to most of its competitors in the struggle for predominance in Anatolia. One example was the opportunity to expand into southeastern Europe (in Ottoman terminology: Rumeli, often Latinized as Rumelia), not only to the territories of the Byzantine Empire, but soon to the Bulgarian, Serbian, and Albanian principalities as well. With Rumelia as a base, Mehmed I and his successors rapidly reconstituted the Ottoman state after Bayezid's defeat under the walls of Ankara in 1402. Without Ottoman possessions in the Balkans this strategy would have been far more difficult, if not impossible.

During the 14th century, Byzantium experienced one succession struggle after another, and both reigning Byzantine emperors and pretenders were quite willing to bring in allies from neighboring polities. From the Byzantine point of view, Muslim neighbors appeared to be less dangerous than the knights, princes, and traders from Catholic Europe, often known as "Franks" or "Latins," who remained in the area even after their short-lived domination of Constantinople (1204-1261) had come to an end. After the Byzantine reconquest of the city, Venetians and Genoese continued to control Mediterranean trade, while parts of the Peloponnesus and numerous Aegean islands still were ruled by "Frankish" dynasties. In 1347, John Kantakuzenos, who had already married one of his daughters to the Ottoman sultan Orhan, made himself the Byzantine emperor after a successful rebellion. Additional Byzantine-Ottoman alliances followed; and these events enabled the Ottoman sultans to create a durable base on the European side of the Sea of Marmara.

One of the major political and ideological advantages arising from the border location of the fledgling Ottoman principality was the attraction it held for many young warriors of Anatolia to participate in military and marauding expeditions in the lands of the "infidels." These warriors, known as *gazis*, were in some instances subjects of neighboring Anatolian principalities; in other words, the Ottoman sultans were able to gain military resources at the expense of their Muslim neighbors. Just like the Christian Crusaders, many Islamic religious warriors easily reconciled their wish to spread the true religion with the prospect of land and spoils.

It is important to keep in mind that in the 14th century, Anatolia was inhabited by numerous nomadic tribes whose quest for pasturelands made them willing to cross over to the Balkan Peninsula. Once these nomads had settled in Rumelia, their tribal structure was soon replaced by a purely military one. We know very little about the processes involved in this momentous changeover. But the militarization of the Rumelian nomads may indicate that although the Ottoman sultans promoted the immigration of Muslim subjects into the Balkan provinces, they also sought to control the newcomers. Faced with the great number of Anatolian principalities founded by nomadic tribes, the sultans must have sought guarantees against future revolts and the creation of independent polities by immigrant tribesmen.

There is little available source material concerning the land acquisition of Turkish nomads in the Balkans. This scarcity of documentation has led to heated debates about population density in the Balkans before the beginning of the Ottoman conquest and the loss in population resulting from the wars that accompanied it. We cannot determine the extent to which the plague epidemics of the late 14th century decimated the population quite independently of war casualties. In any case, roving armies were an ideal vehicle to spread the plague. Historians in the Balkan states sometimes assume that there was a very large resident population before the Ottoman conquest, but this assessment tends to reflect nationalist interests more than anything else. Turkish historians, by contrast, as well as many Ottomanists the world over, put the numbers far lower. However, the sources allow for nothing but educated guesses.

Army and Administration

The Ottomans' rapid conquests were possible only because they had developed an efficient military structure. Warfare in the 14th and 15th centuries was conducted primarily on horseback and with swords, lances, and sabers. Ottoman horsemen were financed by so-called *timars*, allocations from mostly rural taxes, distributed by the sultans' financial administration. The holder of a *timar* was obliged to appear mounted for military campaigns, and if his *timar* was large enough, to bring along an appropriate number of armed men. He had to pay for horses and weapons himself.

At first glance the *timar* would appear to resemble the medieval European fief, and the two institutions do have several common characteristics. In both cases the taxes came from village populations that managed their family farms independently; the "home farm" of the *timar* holder, who held this supplementary resource until well into the 16th century, never had more than a secondary role. Also, both social systems had a relatively small amount of cash in circulation, but the *timars* did not function within a barter economy. Even in the 15th century—there are no sources available for earlier periods—*timar* holders could maintain themselves only when there was a market nearby where they could stock up on horses and weapons. There is no record of craftsmen serving on a rural estate in the Ottoman Empire, as there were in several periods and places in European history.

There were other significant differences between the *timar* and the European-style fief. Ottoman law had no equivalent of a *commendatio*, in which an individual placed himself under the protection of an overlord and pledged his loyalty to him, nor was there a hierarchical pyramid with a highest feudal lord in command of less powerful feudatories, who in turn served as feudal lords of less powerful underlings, and so forth. Apart from slaves, all working people were direct subjects of the sultan (*reaya*), but they were clearly subordinate to the privileged imperial administrators (*askeri*), which included both judges (*kadıs*) and *timar* holders.

While in many parts of medieval Europe feudatories judged their subordinate peasants and thus might be both party and judge, courts presided over by *timar* holders were unknown in the Ottoman Empire; in certain cases even slaves addressed the *kadı*. *Timar* holders furthermore rarely had a chance to put down roots and turn into local aristocrats, as was often the case with officials that medieval Europeen kings sent into the countryside: after all, *timar* holders were transferred from one region to another too frequently. Thus the centralized Ottoman state of the 15th and 16th centuries wielded far more power over its "feudal" cavalrymen than the pre-absolutist European kingdoms over their dukes, counts, and knights.

Recruited originally from the fifth of all war prisoners that the sultan was entitled to after every military campaign, the janissaries (Ottoman *yeniçeri*, new army) were by far the best known foot soldiers. Later, when this source of recruitment no longer sufficed, a large percentage of janissaries consisted of forcibly recruited sons of Christian peasants who were already subjects of the sultan. The secondary literature refers to this form of recruitment as "levy of boys" (*devşirme*). This same procedure was also used to select future high-level administrators. In this case, the boys were given a thorough education in the school of pages situated in the sultans' palace. As for the future soldiers, they were sent to Anatolia to serve local peasants, and there they were expected to convert to Islam and learn the Turkish language. At some point they were sent to the capital, where they were known as "novice boys" (Turkish: *acemi oğlan*) and waited for a place to free up in the ranks of the janissaries.

Until the mid-16th century, janissaries officially were not allowed to marry during their active service. They were entitled to do so only when as mature men, they had been discharged from the service of the sultan. Of course it is difficult to determine how far this regulation was complied with in practice. Moreover, any member of the janissaries or *timar* holder was a privileged servitor of the sultan. This meant not only immunity from taxation, but in the case of the janissaries also the right to be judged only by one's own commanding officer. Particularly in provincial towns a janissary often commanded great respect.

Janissaries and other office-holders of the sultan were so dependent on him that their condition bore a resemblance to slavery. In this regard, the levy of boys was in line with the medieval Near Eastern tradition of using slaves or former slaves of the ruler for military functions. The loyalty of foreign-born soldiers to their sultan, who had made possible their often substantial social ascent, was, from the perspective of the rulers, the chief attraction of this institution. For the strict exegetes of religious law, janissaries posed a problem, because these men were of course not foreign, but subjects of the sultan. On the other hand, no one who lived in an Islamic state could be enslaved, no matter what his religion, unless he was a non-Muslim and had tried to throw off Ottoman rule. But no one claimed that the conscripts or their families had done any such thing. One way around the difficulty was the argument that janissaries and other servants of the sultan were not slaves, but only appointed to serve the sultan. Even so, in the 16th century, at least in Egypt, free Ottoman subjects were known to refuse to take orders from an office-holder of the sultan whom they regarded as a mere slave.

Moreover, the Ottoman state maintained irregular troops whose job it was to spread terror and confusion as vanguard *akıncı* (raiders). Some of these units, known as *martolos,* were made up of Christians. The nomads of the Balkan Peninsula did their military service in shifts; while a limited number of men actively participated in any given campaign, the remaining members of their unit, called an *ocak*, were in charge of supplies. Peasant soldiers (*müsellem*) were another 15th-century group to serve the army without cash payment. They were rewarded for their service with tax exemptions on their farms in Anatolian villages.

At least since the time of Mehmed II the Ottoman units from the provinces were usually commanded by men who had completed their course of study at the palace school and had been sent to the provinces as military commanders and then as governors. As governors also served in the army, they were often away from the places they had been assigned to and which supplied the taxes needed to finance their activities. In the highest ranks of the administration and the military were the viziers, who convened on a regular basis. This imperial council (*divan-ı humayun*) supported the ruler in running the empire, and it issued orders in his name.

In battle the early sultans employed strategies which allowed them to continually best European feudal armies. There was just one commander in chief—in the period from 1300 to 1481 it was generally the sultan himself. Subordinate commanding officers were famous for the discipline with which they stuck to a fixed battle plan. European armies, by contrast, were mostly a conglomerate of independent forces, and it often happened that at the first sign of trouble, the mutually exclusive interests of the allies made the battle formation fall apart; the defeat at Nicopolis in 1396 is only one example among many. Moreover, European military leaders seem to have been tricked each and every time by the same Ottoman ruse. The Europeans would follow a relatively small group of Ottoman soldiers supposedly on the run, only to find, to their great surprise, that they had ended up in a trap where they were confronted with a well-organized main army commanded by the sultan. As a result the Ottoman armies of the 15th century had a reputation for virtual invincibility.

The Islam of the Early Ottomans

Most Turks who arrived in the Balkans were already Muslims. The Gagauz people, who still reside in Romania today, were an exception. These people appear to have immigrated in the 13th century, that is, in the pre-Ottoman epoch, and became Orthodox Christians. Of course, when considering nomadic groups or even members of the court of Sultans Osman or Orhan, we should not overestimate their knowledge of or compliance with Islamic customs. Thus the Moroccan world traveler Ibn Battuta (1304-1368/69 or 1377)[1] was received by Orhan's wife when he visited the royal residence, since the sultan himself was away at the time. In later centuries, a gesture of this sort would have been unthinkable. As far as the religion of the nomads is concerned, the origins of their numerous practices of non-Islamic origin are still disputed. Some experts emphasize the role of shamanism, while others focus on nature cults. In the folk Islam of rural Anatolia, rock formations and ancient trees were often associated with the miracles of saints.

While the urban high Islam of the legal and religious scholars (*ulema*) left no room for practices of this kind, some dervish communities were quite flexible. It can be assumed that the early Ottoman sultans had a friendly relationship with these somewhat heterodox sheikhs. Fifteenth-century chronicles report that a sheikh named Edebali prophesied that Sultan Osman I, after whom the dynasty was named, would rule the entire world, and the holy man gave his daughter to the prince in marriage. Edebali, in turn, seems to have been one of the rather large numbers of sheikhs who were heavily involved in a revolt of nomads, which was crushed in 1240 with a great deal of bloodshed by the current Seljuk sultan, with the aid of Frankish mercenaries. One of these mercenaries reported his adventures to the Dominican Simon of St. Quentin; his report is one of the few sources for this revolt that has come down to us. Another sheikh from the same milieu, whose followers would play a major role in Ottoman history, was Hacı Bektaş, who had escaped Seljuk persecution by fleeing to a remote central Anatolian village. It would appear that since the mid-14th century this sheikh, about whose life on earth hardly anything is known, was regarded as the patron of the most famous Ottoman corps, the janissaries. His legendary *Vita*, dating at least in part to the late 1400s or early 1500s, is one of the important documents of Anatolian cultural history.

Dervishes also had an important role in the Turkish settlement of Rumelia and the Islamization of the local population. It often happened that a religious leader known as *Baba* (father) would settle in a sparsely populated area and gather followers. After his death, his grave was venerated by the local residents, who hoped that his intercession would yield good harvests, heal illnesses, and ensure ample offspring. Donations enabled the dervishes to construct sometimes quite elaborate lodges. In Anatolia these institutions often dated back to earlier Muslim rulers, and the Ottoman sultans generally respected them and sometimes even increased the endowments. In Ottoman times dervish lodges were obliged to shelter travelers overnight so that official aid was likely to safeguard travel routes. Several Ottoman sultans apparently intended to advance the Islamization of Christian peasants and heterodox nomads by supporting dervishes who were willing to promote Sunnite right belief.

The Ottoman sultans also lent their support to urban high Islam, most notably by constructing mosques and schools (*medrese*) to teach Islamic law and theology and to train future scholars of jurisprudence and theology (*ulema*). Since Islam has no priests, it fell to these specialists to guide believers in the proper practice of their religion. Since it was assumed that God would not allow the entire community of Muslims to be misled, once the *ulema* had reached a consensus, their decisions were binding for all believers. Mosques and *medrese*s were often combined to form larger complexes (*külliye*) with guest houses for traveling dervishes, soup kitchens, and schools for young children. Generally the donors, who were often sultans, princes, and princesses, arranged to be buried near these buildings. The foundation administrators were responsible for paying salaries to the relevant employees, including the legal and religious experts who taught in the *medrese*s. Exceptional scholars in this still quite rustic society soon aroused the interest of the sultans. Sheikh Bedreddin, who was both a mystic and a scholar of law, acted as an army judge for Prince Musa, one of the sons of Bayezid I who lost out in the struggle for succession. After a later unsuccessful revolt that his grandson and apologist claimed had never happened, the sheikh was hanged in Serres at the order of Mehmed I in 1417.

A New City, a New Polity

The transformation of Istanbul into an Ottoman city, with a strong Muslim presence, was one of the priorities that Sultan Mehmed the Conqueror seems to have set for himself. First the Hagia Sophia (Aya Sofya), now converted into a mosque, served as the religious center of the city. A *medrese* was added on so that theology, jurisprudence, and other subjects could be taught. In 1463 Mehmed II also began building a large complex that consisted of a mosque, sixteen *medreses*, a special school for Koran recitation, and other institutions. The buildings were located on the site of the Church of the Holy Apostles, which had been torn down for this purpose. In choosing a location for his royal residence, Mehmed II appears to have hesitated between Istanbul and Edirne, and he had large palace complexes built in both cities: the Eski Saray in Istanbul, the current site of the Suleiman Mosque and the central building of the University of Istanbul, and the Topkapı Palace, which still exists today. The palace in Edirne was blown up by an Ottoman general during the Balkan War of 1877, but until the early 18th century, it was used extensively by many sultans, especially during the hunting season.

Trade was an important complement to courtly life and Islamic high culture. In the late Byzantine era, the tiny city of Galata, with its mostly Genoese merchants, had become the economic center of the region; Mehmed II relocated it to the southern shore of the Golden Horn, where two covered bazaars (called *bedesten*) were set up on a hill, and formed the centerpiece of the present-day Grand Bazaar. Valuable wares were traded here, and Mehmed II's Grand Vizier Mahmud Paşa built a mosque nearby.

The lack of people was a major problem. Many had fled before the siege, and during the three-day rampage of the soldiery just after the conquest there were further losses. Now a time limit was set within which the refugees could benefit from amnesty and retake possession of their homes. To promote immigration from the old Ottoman provinces, new residents were promised home ownership, a pledge that was later retracted. Certain provinces had to send specified numbers of new settlers to Istanbul. These people (*sürgün*) were not allowed to leave the city to which they had been assigned, although otherwise they retained the rights of freemen. While quite a few of these immigrants were Christians, there were enough Muslims among them to give the city an Islamic character. Evidently courtiers were encouraged or perhaps even ordered to establish mosques in Istanbul that soon became the nuclei for new town quarters.

These new regulations transformed the lives of many Ottoman subjects. They were especially burdensome for those *sürgün* who had been sent to Istanbul against their will. The first recorded documentation of dissatisfaction with the policies of Mehmed II dates to his successor, Bayezid II (1481-1512). In the opponents' perspective, the old capital of the Roman emperors was a cursed place at which even King Solomon had fallen victim to the temptations of polytheism; despite its universal reputation for sanctity even the Aya Sofya was considered unable to dispel this curse.

Changes in the relationship of the sultan to his subjects also made for dissatisfaction. Peasants were obliged to pay higher taxes for the campaigns and conquests of Sultan Mehmed II; there is no record of their feelings on this subject. We have more information about the ways in which upper-class Anatolian families forfeited their privileged positions: until the time of Mehmed II, some members of the Anatolian aristocracies had held important positions in the Ottoman administration, but Mehmed II made it much harder for them to do so. The sultan preferred to fill high-level posts with men who had been trained in the school of pages at the palace and whose dependency on his person strongly resembled slavery. This way, the ruler could have office-holders executed without appealing to a court, and take over their assets after their deaths. The growing distance between the sultan and his court was also reflected in the fact that the first known regulation of court protocol, establishing a strict hierarchy of the dignitaries concerned, stems from the time of Mehmed the Conqueror. Over time, this text was revised and in the 16th century made even stricter.

Boys who had come to Istanbul either as prisoners of war or by way of the levy of boys and seemed especially talented were accepted into the school of pages. These young people were placed in a strict hierarchy, with those highest up rendering personal services to the ruler as pages. During the reign of Mehmed II, the sultan did not reside in the harem, as was common from the second half of the 16th century onwards, but in the third court of the palace surrounded by his pages. When a young man had finished his schooling, the palace arranged for him to be married, often to a woman who had been raised in the harem of the sultan. Beginning with the reign of Mehmed II, those who proved their abilities as military officers and adminstrators in the provinces could count on being brought back to the capital and appointed to high public office; the most sucessful might even become grand viziers.

Mehmed II introduced a new rule that brought about drastic changes in courtly life. He mandated that after a sultan had acceded to the throne, he should have his brothers murdered to avoid long civil wars. This practice lasted until the beginning of the 17th century. At this time there was no regulation comparable to primogeniture; in principle at least all sons of a ruling sultan were equally entitled to the succession; however, as most sultans did not live very long by our standards the eldest son might well be the only adult and thus have an advantage over his younger brothers. To prepare for their position, princes were sent to the provinces, typically accompanied by their mother and a mentor known as a *lala*. As soon as they were old enough, they began courting allies who would later support them as candidates for the throne. Anyone who could win over the janissaries to his side normally had the best chance. As a result, the battle for succession to the throne was not only institutionalized, but carried to an extreme; in order to survive, all princes had to do everything in their power to become the next sultan. If the ruler reached a relatively advanced age, the battle for succession took place during his lifetime and sometimes with his participation.

Contemporaries such as Aşıkpaşazade, a chronicler descended from an old dervish family in Central Anatolia, were evidently wary of these developments and of the courtly culture that accompanied it.

Aşıkpaşazade's chronicle, which he wrote during the second half of the 15th century when he was an old man, by contrast emphasized the simple life and the accessibility of the early Ottoman sultans.

Towards the end of his reign, Mehmed II made yet another attempt to weaken the power base of the established Anatolian families, many of whose members received a portion of their income from pious foundations instituted by their forebears. These foundations served a religious and charitable purpose, and were managed by trustees, who often were descended from the family of the donor and had a certain amount of leeway in administering the assets. From the perspective of the donors, this procedure had the advantage of circumventing the prescriptions of the Islamic law of inheritance, which provides for a distribution among many beneficiaries. As we have already seen, several of these pious foundations stemmed from pre-Ottoman times, but were confirmed after the Ottoman conquest.

Mehmed II now took a step that came into clear conflict with Islamic law governing pious foundations. In his later years he confiscated numerous institutions that he had previously approved, and changed the legal status of their property into *timars*. Apart from the effects upon the donor families, Mehmed II's policies must have hurt many ordinary subjects as well, since travelers, students, and pilgrims were the usual beneficiaries of pious foundations. When Mehmed II died in 1481, his son and successor Bayezid II was embroiled in a fierce battle for succession with his brother Cem and quickly reversed this policy.

CHAPTER 2

◆ ◆ ◆

Between East and West
(1481-1600)

Consolidation under Bayezid II

Under Bayezid II, the Ottoman Empire experienced a phase of consolidation, despite several wars with Venice, Poland, and the Mamluk sultans. Ottoman control of the Black Sea coasts was made complete by the conquest of the port towns of Akkerman (Belgorod-Dnestrovskij/Ukraine) and Kilia (Kilija/ Ukraine). In the 16th century, the Black Sea, now a purely Ottoman lake, was off limits to foreign ships, and its coastal areas served only to provide the rapidly growing capital of Istanbul with food and other necessities. Moreover, Montenegro came under Ottoman sovereignty, although this addition cannot have been very significant, considering the poverty and remoteness of the area.

From an economic point of view, the more significant development was the immigration of Spanish and later Portuguese Jews, which began in 1492 with their expulsion from Spain by Ferdinand and Isabella. Those who came directly from Spain had to leave behind their assets and could bring along only their business contacts. Many so-called Marranos, baptized Jews who secretly retained their religion, also had to flee from the Inquisition in the 16th century; but as Christians moving to a Christian land, they could salvage substantial portions of their assets. Typically these people thus reached the Ottoman domains in several stages. The new immigrants were settled in Istanbul, where the Greek-speaking Jews had been brought together under Mehmed II, and in Salonika. In the latter city the Spanish Jews made the manufacture of woolen cloth into a regional industry; the cloth was milled outside the city. The state assigned them the manufacture of fabric for the janissaries' uniforms. Additionally, around 1493, the immigrants established the first functioning printing press in the Ottoman Empire.

The Ottoman Sultans in the Near East (1481-1600)

The long war between Bayezid II and the Mamluk sultans (1484-1491) brought no decisive gains. In the place of Uzun Hasan, the prince of the Ak-koyunlu Turkmen defeated by Mehmed II, a youthful sheikh of the Safaviyeh Sufi order established himself as Shah Ismail I in 1500. Shah Ismail conquered Baghdad in 1504. In the vicinity of the eastern Anatolian town of Erzincan, the Ottoman sultanate now had a border in common with this new and ambitious ruler. Even more threatening was the attraction that the newly established polity held for the politically and militarily marginalized nomads of Anatolia. In 1511 followers of Shah Ismail rebelled against Ottoman rule deep in southwestern Anatolia and enjoyed some initial success. The crisis of the Empire was aggravated by the succession struggle between the sons of Bayezid II in 1512; in the course of these disputes, Prince Selim forced his father to abdicate, killed his brothers, and acceded to the Ottoman throne as Selim I (1512-1520).

The eight-year reign of Selim I brought rapid expansion, although this time it was in the Middle East rather than in the Balkans. After an extremely bloody suppression of the Anatolian followers of Shah Ismail, Selim defeated him in 1514 at Çaldıran and advanced as far as western Iran. Even so, the janissaries refused to follow the sultan on a campaign farther east.

The Ottoman takeover of the Mamluk state only took slightly over a year; in 1516 the campaign began with the conquest of the city of Diyarbekir in southeastern Anatolia, and in the same year the Mamluk ruler Kansuh al-Ghuri fell in the battle at Marj Dabik. His successor Tumanbay tried to refuse Selim I access to Cairo; but after the lost Battle of Raydaniyya the last Mamluk sultan was hanged in front of a gate to his capital in 1517. The Sharif of Mecca offered his submission, and Selim I showed his appreciation by allocating important Egyptian resources to support the population of the Hijaz, thus indirectly underwriting the Muslim pilgrimage to Mecca. Now the power of the Ottoman sultan extended into the southern Red Sea, except that control over Yemen remained limited, and Ottoman rule in this territory was essentially confined to the cities until its collapse in the 1630s.

Selim I's conquests created an altogether new type of empire. Now the Ottoman realm was no longer limited to the Balkans and Anatolia and thus situated at the edge of the Islamic world. On the contrary, it now comprised the old heartlands, including the cities of Cairo, Aleppo, and Damascus. The Ottoman conquest marked a turning point in the way Syria was ruled; henceforth these provinces were no longer administered from Cairo, but rather from Istanbul. Even so, local families from Mamluk times, often resident in fortified houses at the edge of the desert, remained prominent. As for Egypt, the Mamluks continued to play a role in provincial government. It remained relatively common until the early 19th century to import young military slaves, who after training and emancipation formed a kind of local aristocracy that collected taxes in town and country. While Mamluk recruitment had been going on for centuries, there was a significant difference between the pre-Ottoman and the Ottoman epochs: after 1517 the ruler no longer emerged from among the Mamluks, and the latter had to function within an Ottoman framework, determined by the central government.

After 1517, Cairo sank to the level of a provincial city, but recent research has shown that in the 16th and 17th centuries a great deal of money was earned there and spent on magnificent urban palaces, commercial centers, and shopping streets. In addition, trade with India was blossoming, and the import of spices, dyes, and printed cotton fabrics enabled some merchants to amass considerable wealth. Coffee, originating from Abyssinia and Yemen, became popular in the mid-16th century, first in Egypt and then in Istanbul and Anatolia. The trade in coffee was also profitable, although during the 17th century this beverage was prohibited several times.[1] Coffee and spice traders could make quite a lot of money, because they dealt in goods that were not everyday or military necessities, and were therefore exempt from the strict state supervision governing the grain merchants and butchers of Istanbul. Also, these Cairo merchants proved that at least in Egypt, money could be earned and passed down to the next generation without the intervention of the central government. In the Ottoman heartlands such opportunities were far more limited. It is therefore important not to lump together developments in the various Ottoman provinces.

In the course of the 16th century, the sultan expanded his power along the North African coast west of Cairo as well. Hayreddin Barbarossa, a corsair from the island of Midilli (Lesbos) established his power base in present-day Algeria; he later submitted to the authority of Selim I's successor Suleiman the Magnificent and was appointed governor of the new province. In 1534 he advanced to commander-in-chief of the Ottoman fleet and soon thereafter conquered Tunis, which, due to the immigration of Spanish Muslims, became an important center of trade and industry. A long campaign by Suleiman the Magnificent in 1533-1536 resulted in both a brief occupation of Tabriz and the incorporation of Iraq into the Ottoman Empire, including the key cities of Mosul, Baghdad, and Basra.

Expansion in Europe during the 16th Century

Suleiman the Magnificent's accession to the throne in 1520 brought a renewed expansion westward. In 1521, the Ottomans captured Belgrade, which had been besieged unsuccessfully by Mehmed the Conqueror, and in 1526 the Battle of Mohács ended with the defeat of the Hungarian army and the death of King Lajos II. Suleiman first appointed a local nobleman named John Zapolya as king, in accordance with standard practice following Ottoman conquests, which often involved a transitional period of local rule before direct government was introduced. But Zapolya died soon thereafter, and the Habsburg King Ferdinand I asserted claims to his inheritance and appeared with an army in Hungary. A long Ottoman-Habsburg war ensued. After Sultan Suleiman's conquest of important fortresses (Pécs, Sikós, Gran), the greater portion of Hungary became an Ottoman province between 1541 and 1547, with the capital in the old royal city of Buda. Transylvania remained a separate principality under Ottoman suzerainty but was ruled by local princes, while a narrow strip of western Hungary came under Habsburg rule. In the course of this war, Vienna was besieged in 1529. Contrary to the initial expectations at the sultan's court, the Ottoman sphere of influence had more or less attained its maximal westward expansion by the mid-1500s, and Hungary became a border area for one and a half centuries.

In the Mediterranean region, the Ottoman Empire expanded significantly when it conquered the island of Cyprus in 1571; even the victory of Lepanto by the united Spanish and Venetian fleets in 1573 did little to reverse Ottoman progress. This island, valuable because of its cotton and sugar plantations, had belonged to the Venetian colonial empire since the beginning of the 16th century. The Ottoman administration lost no time in bringing in settlers from Anatolia, primarily poor peasants and members of the religious sect of the Kızılbaş (known as "redheads" because of their preferred head covering), which the Sunnis considered heretical.[2] As townsmen and villagers in southern Anatolia could designate those people from amongst their midst that were to be sent off to populate the island, in the early stages of Ottoman domination Cyprus seems to have functioned as a place where outcasts were banished.

The Expansion of Diplomatic Relations

Even after the death of Selim I (1520) and Shah Ismail (1524), war was frequent between Iran and the Ottoman Empire throughout the 16th century. But in the peaceful intervals there were political relations as well. An ongoing point of discussion was the desire of Shiite pilgrims to visit not only Mecca and Medina, but also the graves of the descendants of the Prophet Muhammad, most of which were in Iraq. However, Ottoman authorities feared that these pilgrimages provided opportunities for espionage. There was only limited contact with the other great empire of the Islamic world, namely that of the

Mughal dynasty, which had ruled northern India since 1526. This contact focused primarily on the holy cities of Mecca and Medina, which were also visited by numerous Indian pilgrims.

Suleiman the Magnificent found a European ally in Francis I, king of France, who, following his defeat in the battle of Pavia in 1525, could return to his throne only after paying a hefty ransom to his opponent, the Habsburg Emperor Charles V. Accordingly, the alliance between king and sultan had an anti-Habsburg thrust and in 1543, an Ottoman-French fleet captured Nice from the Duke of Savoy, then an ally of the emperor. French ambassadors appeared in Istanbul, the first permanently accredited legation after the Venetian. Until the late 18th century, Ottoman-French alliances were revived periodically whenever it seemed advantageous in facing their common enemy, the Habsburgs.

At the very end of the 16th century, English merchants began to do business on Ottoman territory, and sought to oust their Venetian competitors from their traditional waterways, even resorting to piracy in the process. There had been relations between Sultan Murad III (r. 1574-1595) and Queen Elizabeth I since 1580. The Ottomans were especially interested in English tin, used in the manufacture of armaments. English deep-sea vessels that the sultans hoped to "charter" when required may have played a role in the Ottoman interest in this remote kingdom as well. The basis for this relationship, cemented at one point by correspondence between Queen Elizabeth I and Murad's consort Safiye Sultan, was unquestionably the battle against the Habsburgs. The defeat of the Spanish Armada in 1588 made it clear that the war against the English Queen required significant resources on the part of King Philip II of Spain that thus could not be used against the Ottomans. The English also capitalized on the motive of a broad common front against Catholicism.

The status of envoys in residence and of merchants was regulated by so-called *ahidname*, which European historiography calls "capitulations." For the most part, they were privileges granted unilaterally by a sultan to the subjects of a ruler with whom he was on friendly terms, intended to improve relations with actual or potential adversaries of the Habsburg Empire. The capitulations were valid only during the lifetime of the sultan who had issued them, and had to be submitted to the successor for reconfirmation. These privileges set the amount of customs duties that the subjects of the ruler in question needed to pay. By the end of the 16th century, the Venetians, the French, and the English had been granted these capitulations. In the 18th, 19th, and early 20th centuries, when the balance of power had been reversed to the Ottomans' disadvantage, these capitulations became a real impediment to Ottoman policymaking. But Suleiman the Magnificent and later Murad III, who had granted concessions to the English, could not foresee this consequence.

Ottoman Policy in the Indian Ocean Region (1500-1600)

To understand the extraordinarily successful campaign against the Mamluk Empire, which added a new territorial dimension to the Ottoman realm in 1516-1517, it is useful to consider Portuguese expansion and Indian Ocean trade in the Late Middle Ages. New developments included circumnavigation of the Cape of Good Hope in 1488, the Portguese arrival on the western coast of India in 1498, and the Portuguese occupation of the island of Ormus in the Persian Gulf in 1515. In the course of the 15th century, the Egyptian sultans had tried to compensate for losses in tax revenues caused by the plague epidemics of the time. One such method was to declare the passage of goods from southern Asia a state monopoly; from then on, Venetian and Genoese traders had to buy the goods they wished to export from representatives of the sultan. After the Portuguese had opened up the Cape route to the Indian Ocean, the attempt on the part of their king to monopolize the spice trade for his own benefit resulted in a direct confrontation with the sultans of Egypt and Syria.

The situation was aggravated by the fact that in the course of the Late Middle Ages, pilgrims and long-term residents of Mecca and Medina had become dependent on Egypt for their grain supply. As a consequence, Portuguese incursions into the Red Sea posed a direct threat to an undisturbed pilgrimage. However, the Egyptian rulers lacked a navy. Despite the conflicts of interest in eastern Anatolia, the Mamluk sultan Kansuh al-Ghuri therefore formed an alliance with the Ottomans, who supported him with their fleet in the Red Sea. The collaboration between these unequal partners left much to be desired, however, and Kansuh al-Ghuri's support of Shah Ismail soon supplied a pretext for an attack on the Mamluk realm (1516-1517). It can be assumed that the Ottomans also intended to take control of the lucrative trade in the Red Sea region. Unfortunately, this early "economic policy" of the Ottoman sultans is not well documented.

In any case, the Ottoman rulers tried to exert their influence on the west coast of India as well. In 1538, a large Ottoman fleet appeared before the harbor city of Diu, but there was no confrontation with the Portuguese. In 1552, an Ottoman fleet under the leadership of Piri Reis attempted to conquer the island of Ormus, at that time a Portuguese possession. Piri Reis was an established cartographer and experienced navigator remembered today as the designer of a map of America surviving only in fragments, which is based on work by Columbus that is no longer extant. The operation ended with the loss of the entire fleet; a junior commander named Seydi Ali Reis attempted in vain to rescue some of the ships and wrote a report about the perilous operation he had conducted.[3] No major campaign in the Indian Ocean was organized after this disaster. Still, the Ottomans supplied firearms and artillerymen to various princes who were fighting against the Portuguese in South Asia.

It did not take the Venetians long to realize that the Ottomans were the up-and-coming power in the Red Sea region, and that future spice trading would depend on their goodwill, a consideration which explains why Venice acted cautiously after having lost several bases in the eastern Mediterranean to Mehmed II and Bayezid II. Moreover, Venetian and Ottoman merchants both wished to revitalize the spice trade through the Red Sea. The sultan himself was keenly interested because expanding trade would bring in increased tax revenues. Both sides therefore stood to benefit from the Portuguese failure to monopolize the spice trade via the Indian Ocean and the Cape route. The traditional trade route retained its full significance until the end of the 16th century.

Courtly and Imperial Culture: Architecture and the Fine Arts

As we can see from the building complexes that are still standing today, such as the sultans' mosques in Bursa and Edirne, there was an Ottoman monumental style in architecture as early as the 14th and 15th centuries. In the early 1400s Persian artisans were employed in the decoration of a Bursa mosque. Even so, Mehmed the Conqueror's efforts to develop Istanbul and Edirne into dazzling capitals represented the beginning of a new epoch. The Topkapı Palace includes buildings constructed entirely according to Iranian models, such as Çinili Köşk, which houses a ceramics museum today. On the other hand, the towers of Orta Kapu ('middle gate') and the grand loggia overlooking the sea apparently owe something to Italian models. This eclectic style was evidently intended to highlight Mehmed II's conquests and the fact that his reign was conceived as a world power. The reuse of ancient columns in the court of the mosque of Mehmed II also apparently signified the sultan's status as successor to the Byzantine emperor. Mehmed II seems to have regarded these columns as precious and kept a close eye on the way they were used.

While the eclectic style of Mehmed the Conqueror was abandoned by his successor in favor of a uniformly Ottoman architectural tradition, the appreciation of ancient columns and other workpieces could also be observed in the mid-16th century. A similar frame of mind probably explains certain legends about the Hagia Sophia. This corpus of tales derives only in part from Byzantine and Arab models and also includes innovations from about 1500. Even though these legends at one point in time apparently served to transmit protests against the new-fangled style of the sultan's government, they still contained a rich collection of stories about the famous building that continued to be popular even when the protest against Mehmed the Conqueror's innovations had died down.

The tradition that every sultan build a large mosque complex, including schools and other buildings, usually located in the capital of Istanbul, was followed by nearly all rulers into the early 17th century. In accordance with this tradition, Suleiman the Magnificent, during his long reign, had buildings constructed in the names of family members and in this way allowed them to take part in shaping the face of the capital. In nearly all cases, the same architect was employed, namely Sinan (ca. 1490-1588), head of the corps of the sultan's architects. Sinan also recorded the first Ottoman memoirs by an artist; he dictated the story of his life to one of his friends when he was quite old. These reminiscences indicate that the architect came from a small town near Kayseri and joined the janissary corps through the levy of boys. He must, then, have come from a Christian family, but we know nothing about his Christian name or his ethnicity. In the area in which he grew up, there were Greeks, Armenians, and a Turkophone group of Christians of uncertain origin, the Karamanlıs. In later years Sinan, nicknamed "the old one" on account of his long life, kept in touch with several of his relatives and established a foundation in his homeland, as a provincial native who had attained prominence often did. Sinan's relationship to his patron Sultan Suleiman seems to have been tempestuous at times, but eventually he was granted the high honor of placing his own little mausoleum in the wall of Suleiman's complex. For this reason, Sinan cannot have considered himself as an "anonymous artisan," and his contemporaries did not regard him as such.

Another specifically courtly art cultivated in Istanbul palace circles during the 16th century was miniature painting. Ottoman patrons probably encountered miniatures when they began to acquire books from the Timurid courts of central Asia. However, Ottoman miniature painting was distinguished by the important role accorded to the depiction of historical events, as evident in the illustration of the *Süleyman-name*, which records the official biography of Suleiman the Magnificent in a series of miniatures. Great importance was attached to realistic detail. Artists also used cartography to depict the capital of Istanbul.

Clients outside the court occasionally commissioned goblets, pots, and plates in highly decorated faience, but the design of buildings with large-scale ornamentation of this kind was essentially reserved for sultans and their courtiers. This art was initially an import from the domain of the Timurids, but in the 16th century, Ottoman faience artists developed their own style, characterized by the introduction of red (a previously unknown color) and by the depiction of large flower arrangements with tulips, hyacinths, narcissuses, and peonies on a white background. This art blossomed during the entire 16th century, and its decline after 1600 may be associated with the large-scale import of Chinese porcelain.

The Ottoman State and Its History

The first comprehensive chronicles in the Ottoman language were written in the second half of the 15th century to commemorate the deeds of rulers, so it is no wonder that many chroniclers held high public office at some point in their careers. These chronicles were organized according to the years of a sultan's reign, in much the same way that centuries are the organizational principle of today's history books. Campaigns were the focus of these chronicles, and costly architectural monuments were considered a sign of a ruler's stature.

Another important genre was the treatises of political advice known as "Mirrors for Princes." This genre had a long tradition in the pre-Islamic and Islamic Near East. But beginning in about the mid-1500s, these texts, which could be addressed to sultans or viziers, served as an arena for various groups within the state administration to debate their differences. For example, Lütfi Paşa, a former grand vizier of Suleiman the Magnificent, wrote a "vizier book" (*Asafname*). To put this book's advice in the proper perspective, it is interesting to note that Lütfi Paşa had lost his office because he had been abusive to his wife, who was the sultan's sister; she had reproached him severely for the cruel punishment of another woman.

But the most famous of these books of advice for the leaders of the

Ottoman government is without a doubt the text written by Mustafa Ali from Gallipoli (1541-1600). Ali was a well-educated and extremely experienced man who was unable to realize his "dream career" and never got over this disappointment even though he was appointed to prestigious offices that carried substantial responsibility. However his frustration seems to have spurred his productivity. He wrote a major historical treatise, which was evidently intended mainly for his own reading pleasure and perhaps for a few close friends. Only a small portion of this work has been seriously analyzed to date, but available studies include a perceptive and highly critical biography of Sultan Murad III, whom Ali reproaches for being irresponsible and gullible. In Ali's eyes these failings were especially serious because in Anatolia and Rumelia, Islamic high culture was still a "delicate flower" that needed to acclimatize, and it was incumbent on the ruler to foster this culture. Ali's commentary on the turmoil resulting from the 1595 murder of the many sons of Murad III in Istanbul, many of whom were still children, is especially striking. Ali contends that since the sultan could have predicted what would happen to his descendants after his death, he should not have produced so many children in the first place.[4]

In the 15th century, several chronicles were written in the language of educated contemporaries. However, by about 1500, an artificial language emerged that essentially retained the Turkish syntax, but introduced words and word formations of Arabic and Persian origin. Depending on the situation, this language could be made more Arabic or more Iranian; the Ottoman educated class had a choice of various "pitches." In addition to this courtly mode of expression, there were writings for people who did not speak the elevated form of the language but were literate nonetheless; the prime examples are the aforementioned saints' lives.

Ottoman Sultans as Defenders of Sunni Islam

Courtly art was certainly conceived as a legitimation for the ruler, presenting the sultan to the members of his court as a patron of art and literature and, first and foremost, as a victor in the battle against infidels and Shiites. Parallels were constructed between these two adversaries: Ebusuud Efendi, the highest legal scholar of Suleiman the Magnificent, even thought that the Shiites of Iran should not be regarded as Muslims, and other men of religion followed in his wake. This role of the sultan as a defender of Sunnite "right belief" was made visible to a wider audience by decorating the Süleymaniye with inscriptions that identified the building as a triumph over the Shiite enemy. A panegyrist of the early 1600s also praised the mosque of Sultan Ahmed I, inaugurated in 1617, in this manner.

Non-Ottoman observers were also targeted by this propaganda for the ruler. As we have seen, once Hijas had become part of the Ottoman Empire, the sultans took over the protection of the pilgrims to Mecca. As a result, soldiers had to be made available to accompany the pilgrim caravans through the desert. Even more costly was the fact that from at least the 12th century onwards, the Bedouins of the Syrian, Egyptian, and Arab deserts had to be paid with money and goods to grant pilgrims free passage. Moreover, in the first half of the 16th century, an expensive plan for urban development in Mecca and Medina was undertaken and continued through the 1500s and early 1600s. All these projects were regarded as urgent, in part because the Mughal rulers of northern India were sponsoring the pilgrimage from their own territory and went to great lengths to court the Sharifs of Mecca. The large sums of money that were spent to support the pilgrimage were clearly aimed at making the presence of the Ottoman sultan in this remote territory manifest to Indian and other foreign pilgrims.

In this context it is also important to observe Suleiman the Magnificent and his successors' interest in Sunni pilgrims from central Asia. Political conflicts often prevented these people from taking the shortest route via Iran, so the pilgrimage took many years, entailing a detour through Istanbul. When the first conflicts with the Russian tsars occurred in the mid-16th century, the sultans also aimed at keeping access to Mecca open to central Asian pilgrims.

Even more significant were the changes in the education and duties of legal and religious scholars (*ulema*). The training of these professionals, who were of central importance to every Islamic society, had been regarded as a major concern by Ottoman sultans ever since the time of Mehmed II and before; this type of education continued to be fostered by Suleiman the Magnificent as well. Legal and religious scholars were integrated into Ottoman officialdom and promoted according to fixed standards, a state of affairs which had not existed in earlier eras. In the Islamic empires of the Middle Ages neither the sphere of activity nor the training of many *ulema* had been limited to a single state. Since the relevant disciplines were taught and practiced in Arabic, a well-traveled man like Ibn Battuta, who was from Morocco, could easily serve as *kadı* in northern India.

In the early 15th century, outstanding Ottoman scholars still belonged to this network, but beginning in the second half of the century, the training of *ulema*, who were preparing for a supraregional career within the empire, began to take place in Istanbul, Bursa, and Edirne. After 1516-17 the result was a marginalization of scholars from places like Damascus and Cairo. From the 16th century on, to qualify for a position as *kadı*, the candidate had to have completed a precisely defined career path, both as a teacher and as a judge. The highest positions required teaching experience, normally a post at the high schools of the Süleymaniye. By this point, the number of qualified candidates greatly exceeded the number of open slots; short terms of office therefore alternated with long periods of joblessness. Also, family connections and the support of the sultan were often crucial, especially for the highest positions of military judge (*kadıasker*) and top legal authority (*şeyhülislam*).

Ottoman judges applied two kinds of law, namely religious law (*şeriat*) and sultanic law (*kanun*), based on the ruler's decrees. Moreover, locally enforced practices (*örf*), especially in matters pertaining to tax collection, could become Ottoman law. In principle, sultanic law was supposed only to fill in the gaps in religious law, but in practice new legal arguments were rather common. Ottoman law was based on the assumption that all land used as forests, fields, and meadows belonged to the sultan; only houses and gardens were the private property of the subjects. The peasants were hereditary lease-holders and the holders of *timar*s only managers and tax collectors; they did not own the villages that were allocated to them.

One significant feature of Ottoman law was the statute of limita-tions of fifteen years, after which no claims could be made. This statute had been in effect from the 16th century onwards and possi-bly even earlier. The officially sanctioned circumvention of the Isla-mic ban on charging interest, in which many pious foundations took part starting in the late 15th century, and the rationales provided for this circumvention should also be regarded as a facet of sultanic law.

As time went on, the influence of religious law became more and more pervasive; all Ottoman judges were familiar with this law, which formed part of their training: "secular" law schools did not exist until the 19th century. In consequence the *şeriat* acquired a central signifi-cance not just in religious but also in civil life. Nonetheless, the broad authority of the sultan in legislation, and the related ability to create new laws, was a distinguishing feature of the Ottoman state.

Muslims and Non-Muslims

Selim I's conquests had made the Ottoman polity into an empire with a pronounced Muslim majority, and the term "non-Muslim minori-ties" can be applied beginning with his reign. The largest minority group was Greek Orthodox. Members of this group, who might or might not speak Greek as their first language, lived in the Balkans, on the island of Cyprus, and in the Syrian provinces. Egypt was home to the Coptic minority, while in the mountains of eastern Anatolia, some cities in Asia Minor, and the capital of Istabul there were groups of Gregorian Armenians. The Ottoman Empire had a very limited number of Catholic subjects, on the Aegean islands and in

Dalmatia, Bosnia, and Hungary. Only in Hungary and Transylvania were there Protestant (i.e., Calvinist) groups of any significant size.

Among the Jews, the established (Romaniotic) groups played only a minor role in comparison with the new immigrants who came from Spain and Portugal, and sometimes from Italy. There was also an Ashkenazi influx from Central and Eastern Europe; the linguistic and cultural differences were thus quite significant. But by the 16th century, there was clear evidence of assimilation to the Ottoman milieu, including Jewish songs sung to Ottoman tunes. Spanish immigrants used Spanish written in the Hebrew alphabet (*ladino*) in addition to Hebrew, the language of worship.

Scholars long assumed that the institution of *millet*s, religious communities of non-Muslims regulated by bishops, priests, and rabbis, had been introduced as far back as the 15th or 16th century. This assumption is now being questioned. Religious communities, most notably the Orthodox Church, existed right from the beginning and were recognized by the Ottoman sultans. But in the 16th and 17th centuries, the authority of spiritual leaders over their communities often seems to have been quite limited. Research on the early history of the immigrant Jews in particular has shed light on these internal conflicts.

Non-Muslims of any religion paid a poll tax called a *cizye*. Until the end of the 17th century, this tax was sometimes levied on an entire village as a collective payment, but in principle every able-bodied man was required to pay *cizye*. Taxes were on a sliding scale to reflect individual wealth.

Non-Muslims were disadvantaged in the legal arena; for example, they could not testify against Muslims in court. In business this was a serious problem, which many tried to circumvent by registering their transactions with a *kadı* and thereby creating a paper trail. Rules concerning clothing and items of personal use were supposed to make it clear to even a casual passer-by who was a Muslim and who was a Christian or a Jew. The use of the color green was reserved for Muslims, and so were certain kinds of footwear. In addition, non-Muslims were not supposed to ride unless they were traveling, and bearing arms was a Muslim privilege. All these prohibitions were enforced with greater or lesser energy depending on time and place. It was also illegal for non-Muslims to build houses that were higher than those of their Muslim neighbors; sometimes, even long after an Ottoman conquest, a church was confiscated from its community and transformed into a mosque. In order to gather a sufficient number of worshipers in the vicinity of a given Muslim house of prayer, non-Muslims who lived nearby might even be forced to sell their houses and move away. But the practical reality was often more accommodating than the word of the law and the orders of the sultan. Although officials frowned on Muslims and non-Muslims living side by side, they did so for centuries in several Anatolian cities.

Involuntary conversions to Islam were rare, in stark contrast to the situation in the European states of that era, in which the threat of expulsions and even executions enforced religious conformity. Even some slaves were able to resist the pressure to change their religion. Still, the majority of the slaves, as well as the young men who were drafted into the service of the sultan by the levy of boys, had little choice in this matter. Some people who were considered troublemakers for the Ottoman administration were faced with a choice between severe punishment and conversion to Islam.

The overwhelming majority of all conversions appear to have been voluntary, however. There were several motivating factors: first of all, the unending religious disputes between the Greek Orthodox, Catholics, and Protestants were so repulsive to many people in southeastern Europe that they were no longer inclined to believe in a divine mission of the Christian churches. For less contemplative people, there were of course more "secular" reasons. Apart from getting rid of the *cizye*, conversion to Islam opened up possibilities for social advancement, for example in the service of a governor. Some people may simply have preferred to live as "first-class" rather than as "second-class" subjects. Sometimes there were also conversions of entire villages or families, whose reasons can no longer be reconstructed because of a lack of source material. But the significance of the *cizye* as a source of revenue must have kept Ottoman provincial governors and *kadıs* from enforcing the conversion of the "infidels" too vigorously.

Earning a Living: Agriculture and Crafts

The peasants formed the backbone of the tax-paying subject population; if it had been up to the privileged servitors of the sultan, the whole lot of them would have had to remain in this position. In order to leave the village, a peasant needed permission from his *timar* holder—at least in theory. In practice, an exodus to the city, or perhaps to a province with lower taxes, and joining a mercenary troop were certainly viable alternatives. Soldiers who distinguished themselves in a border region stood to be awarded a *timar*. But the status of these men remained uncertain as long as people still recalled their humble beginnings.

The basis of the village organization was the family farm, which was passed down from father to son and managed independently. As a rule—though there were certainly exceptions—a farm was not divided among the heirs, but managed jointly by them. The *timar* holders cannot have contributed much to the day-to-day operations, since they were often absent. But as some taxes were demanded in kind farmers must often have been prevented from varying the composition of their crops. Conflicts arose about the delivery of tax grains and also about services that farmers owed to the local representatives of the sultan, especially in wartime.

Areas with a high agricultural productivity were more the exception than the rule. In both the Balkans and Anatolia, a good portion of the land was mountainous, so the option of using the more effective heavy plow remained quite limited. In most areas farmers had to stick with the light *aratrum*, which only scratched the surface of the earth but did not turn it over. The potentially fertile coastal plains were swampy and barely usable in the summer because of the danger of malaria. On the Anatolian highlands there was a constant water shortage, which necessitated an annual rotation system with fallow land and posed an additional threat to the harvests, not very plentiful even under the best circumstances. In some places the yield amounted to no more than four times the seeds sown. The decades around 1600, in which there were many crop failures in Italy as well, were especially drought-prone. Rivers suitable for navigation were few, and this fact must have made it especially difficult to ensure an adequate food supply even when crop failures were limited to small areas.

In the course of the 16th century, rural population increased substantially, in line with trends throughout the Mediterranean. In territories that were conveniently situated, this increase in population seems to have fostered relatively labor-intensive specialized cultivation; one example would be the silk growing that began about 1600 in the region around Bursa. At the coasts, raisins, grape syrup, lemon juice, and pomegranates were produced for wealthy customers in the capital, although the lion's share of the profits probably flowed into the pockets of merchants and shipping agents. In response to the denser population structure a sizable number of nomads settled down.

In the villages, the major portion of the goods harvested and produced were most likely used for home consumption, for bartering with neighbors, as seeds for future harvests, and for taxes. In any case, we have no information about the paths these products took except when they left the village. We have already seen that a certain number of markets were indispensable for the functioning of the *timars*. But there are indications that in the second half of the 16th century, at least in the coastal Anatolian provinces, the number of markets rose appreciably. Commerce now also took place on summer pastures, where farmers and nomads got together every year, resulting in a growing market orientation. A significant volume of trade also was conducted at country fairs that in the Balkans often were held at the feastdays of the patron saints of the local churches. In the second half of the 16th century, some of these fairs seem to have been visited by so many merchants that they attracted investments by Ottoman viziers. These kinds of gatherings also encouraged the exchange of goods between regions.

Artisan producers were usually organized in guilds. The masters attempted to limit access to their craft as best they could, and claimed that in doing so they were defending consumer interest in high quality goods. When quarrels arose between guild masters, the market supervisor or the *kadı* could be brought in. Cases of this kind were generally decided according to traditional practice, which was normally set down in writing only when disputes were resolved. In cases in which neither religious law nor orders from the sultan provided guidelines, the Ottoman central administration regarded this traditional practice as definitive, and tended to support the demands of established guild masters, ruling, for example, against trainees who wanted to open their own stores or against particularly enterprising craftsmen who tried to expand their market share at the expense of their colleagues.

Trade as a Possible Source of Wealth

The older secondary literature tended to assert that there was a division of labor according to religion in the Ottoman Empire, with the Muslims concentrating on the service of the sultan and agriculture, but limiting their participation in trade to providing supplies for the city of Istanbul, an enterprise which was strictly controlled by the state. But recent research has shown that this assumption is quite mistaken: just as we have noted in the case of religious and political organization (*millet* system), conditions that may have existed in the mid-19th century have simply been superimposed on older periods without any documentary evidence. A late 15th-century register listing customs payments for Black Sea trade shows that Muslim merchants constituted the vast majority of the people paying customs dues. Many Muslims were also active in Bursa at this time, and, as we have seen, 16th-century Cairo was a center of rich Muslim merchants with broad trade networks.

The Ottoman territory did not constitute a single customs unit, and inland duties represented an important source of income for the exchequer. But the points where such dues were collected were limited in number. Furthermore, if violations occurred it was possible to lodge a complaint with the local *kadı*, and, if necessary, in Istanbul;

such recourse against abusive tax collectors also must have stimulated commerce. After 1516, the Syrian trade center of Aleppo in particular experienced a new period of prosperity which resulted in an extensive construction of khans (caravanserais) and covered shopping streets. As we have already observed in the case of Istanbul, cities expanded with the aid of large pious foundations. Examples from the later 16th century include Üsküdar, on the Asian side of the Bosporus, the Thracian town of Lüleburgaz, and the harbor of Payas along the eastern Mediterranean coast.

Moreover, "ideological" reasoning used to legitimate the supposed division of labor on a religious basis simply did not apply to the 15th- and 16th-century situation. The Islamic prohibition on charging interest has been cited in this context: but the latter did not impede money transactions any more than the corresponding prohibition to which the Catholic Church adhered throughout the Middle Ages. It was either circumvented or openly disregarded. To mask the collection of interest, people often "sold" a house, but the seller continued living in it and paid a rent amounting to a specific percentage of the sale price, while retaining the right to eventually "buy back" the property. Even in Anatolian provincial towns, money was lent by a multitude of small investors; women in particular often earned an extra income by doing so. Pious foundations in Istanbul and big cities in Anatolia extended loans with interest. This practice was roundly condemned by strict legal and religious scholars, but Sultan Suleiman's Grand Mufti Ebusuud Efendi felt that the advantages of these money-lending pious foundations for the Muslim community made it reasonable to tolerate them. All these financial sources were used not only for consumer credit, but sometimes for commercial investment as well.

Another "ideological" rationale for the alleged avoidance of foreign trade by Muslim merchants is based on several misconceptions. It is claimed that good Muslims shied away from contact with "infidels" and that this attitude severly restricted their commercial opportunities. But we need to keep in mind that religious regulations that insist on separateness are usually obeyed only by those who can afford to do so. Second, there was the vast area of domestic trade and, especially in Egypt and Syria, of trade with India that could be accomplished without ever coming into contact with "infidels." Although trade with Europe was certainly important, it would be a major mistake to assume that it was as significant in the 16th century as it was to become in the nineteenth. Moreover, Muslim Ottomans quite often did visit Venice, at least in times of peace.

Ottoman merchants of all religions operated in a political environment that limited their opportunities to accumulate capital. The Ottoman administration regarded economic life from the viewpoint of the consumer, and thus gave priority to supplying the urban market with commodities. On the other hand, merchants rarely had direct access to the ruler; the Jewish banker Joseph Nasi, financier of Sultan Selim II (1566-74) and Duke of Naxos, was a rare exception. Urban producers, most of whom were craftsmen with small businesses, had a much tougher time asserting their interests. Although it was considered the duty of the sultan to give the "poor subjects" a chance to earn money, craftsmen were under strict supervision, at least in the capital, and the opportunities to amass wealth were therefore limited.

The Ottoman administration considered the protection of native craftsmen a high priority when their products were needed for the army, the navy, the court, or the capital. For example, the export of leather or cotton was tightly controlled, and in times of war it was stopped altogether. In some businesses that yielded large tax revenues, such as a mohair-processing mill in Ankara, the raw material used by the craftsmen was protected by export bans. But there were no corresponding import bans to protect newly developing areas of production, because the sultan's administration felt that a greater abundance of goods on the market held prices down. In view of keeping the expenditure for wars and building projects within limits, this consideration was given high priority.

The consumer perspective was not even modified by the interests of certain members of the Ottoman upper class, who—sometimes quite actively—got involved in trade and land speculation. One famous example is Rüstem Paşa, the grand vizier and son-in-law of

Suleiman the Magnificent. But an attitude widespread among Ottoman bureaucrats more closely resembled the ideas of the North African historian and social thinker Ibn Khaldun, who held that the subjects could not pay any taxes if the ruler and his privileged inner circle took away their opportunities to earn.

In one regard, the economic attitude of the Ottoman upper class can certainly be compared with that of European potentates of the 16th century, namely when considering the importance attached to gold and silver as the raw material for coinage. In both cases it was assumed that the import of precious metals could be regarded as positive, and the export as negative. The guiding idea was that the state's display of power, that is, its warfare, was possible only when the coffers were full. In Ottoman territory there were some deposits of silver, but very few of gold; the gold came either from Africa by way of Egypt or from European tribute payments. From the mid-16th century on, the "Spanish" silver from America reached the trade centers of Izmir, Salonika, and Aleppo, since the Ottoman trade balance with the European countries was positive and would remain so for centuries to come. The influx of silver contributed here, as elsewhere, to a rise in price. How great this increase was, however, is difficult to determine because the secular trend since Roman times had been for precious metals to be siphoned off to South Asia. The Ottoman sultans of the 16th century made every effort to stop this depletion, but the large sums that they paid each year to support the pilgrimage to Mecca and Medina must have greatly facilitated the import of Indian goods and thus an outflow of money as an unintended consequence.

CHAPTER 3

◆ ◆ ◆

Hard-Earned Successes and Serious Setbacks (ca. 1600-1774)

Mercenaries, "Zealots," and State Dignitaries

At the end of the 16th century and the beginning of the 17th, the sultans' control over Anatolia was seriously compromised. Sizable gangs of armed men who claimed—with more or less justification—to be serving the ruler or one of his governors ravaged the country. In response the sultans allowed villagers to create militias and in emergencies to refuse outsiders access to their settlements. But this measure was of only limited effectiveness, in part because so many armed people actually did serve one office-holder or another and thus had the power to enforce their demands.

Very few of the rebelling mercenary leaders seem to have planned to form independent polities. Normally the leaders of insurgent troops were quite willing to accept an assignment at the border and thus join the Ottoman governing system. We have scant information as to what simple mercenaries hoped to gain from rebellions of this kind. But it stands to reason that they wanted to trade their uncertain status for the tax exemptions and other privileges that the janissaries enjoyed. The large-scale looting campaigns of these mercenaries, who even briefly occupied important cities in Anatolia including Bursa and Urfa, interrupted trade routes and hence forced some bazaars to shut down.

The use of portable firearms in waging war was on the rise, and the cavalry's reliance on swords and sabers was diminishing. For the *timar* holders who had always fought with swords, on horseback, this often meant a major loss of income and status. The Ottoman state did not try to develop any central organization for the new weaponry and thereby enable the "retrained" cavalrymen to assume a new role. Instead the state relied on a kind of "private initiative," putting

Ottoman administrators in charge of recruiting troops.

Ottoman governors thus employed their own armed militias to collect taxes in their provinces and put a stop to robbers. However, these troops were frequently replaced, and since each new administrator brought along his own mercenaries, the number of unemployed armed men was quite high. In some cases the soldiers appear to have pressured their commander to rebel, so as not to lose their employment. While the number of mercenary leaders operating on their own initiative decreased after about 1630-40, rebellions by soldiers under the leadership of a vizier or pasha occurred throughout the 17th century.

The civil wars of the 1600s were further aggravated by the increasing political activity of the janissaries and other troops stationed in Istanbul, Cairo, and Damascus. Their activity was prompted in part by their uncertain financial circumstances. Like many European sovereigns of their time the Ottoman sultans of the 17th century lacked the means to pay a large standing army on an ongoing basis. Debasing the coinage was one of the common means of covering expenses when the treasury was nearly empty. As a result, soldiers and officers lost buying power, and tried to recoup their losses by stirring up rebellions. During the 17th century, these rebellions often had dire consequences for grand viziers, who stood to lose their heads, and sultans, who could lose their thrones. But tactics of this kind had only a temporary effect; in the long run, the soldiers had no choice but to seek out additional sources of income in the cities where they were stationed.

In some cases, janissaries and others engaged in crafts "on the side." But at least in the case of Cairo, which has been quite thoroughly examined, it was far more common for soldiers to declare themselves "protectors" of craftsmen and merchants and to demand compensation. Sometimes regular protection money was paid over, but often Muslim craftsmen were offered the opportunity to sign up as members of a military corps. In the long run, these units were downgraded to militias by the influx of craftsmen with no previous military training.

Since the privileges of a militiaman included tax exemptions, there were sound economic reasons for artisans to join up. Particularly in Cairo, the militias protected the interests of the craftsmen. However, when after 1750 these units lost power in comparison with Mamluk households, the tax pressure mounted to the point that the daily existence of the lower classes became quite shaky.

Explosive situations in the capital could quite easily result from alliances between military officers, dissatisfied men of religion, and palace dignitaries. These situations were further aggravated by the social situation of many Istanbul residents. In apparent reaction to the economic and political difficulties that "little people" so often had to suffer in the 17th century, a movement took hold in the capital that preached a return to the simplicity of the original Islam. Displays of wealth often triggered loud protests, as did the circumvention of the ban on charging interest and the use of coffee and tobacco. This movement considered the religious practices of many dervish orders, especially the whirling dances of the Mevlevis, abhorrent novelties. Murad IV formed an alliance with members of this movement and tried to make his subjects follow their teachings—without doing so himself. However, after the death of this sultan in 1640, the Ottoman upper class was more inclined to neutralize the leaders of this movement by appointing them to high positions, or by simply banning them from the capital.

The Restoration of the Köprülüs

Mehmed Köprülü, who was appointed grand vizier by Mehmed IV in 1656, preferred to take the latter route. Taking office in the middle of a war with Venice that was going badly for the sultan's navy, the ruler granted him extraordinary authority to avert this crisis. Despite his advanced age, Mehmed Köprülü proved to be a successful officer who in 1657 reconquered two Aegean islands that had recently been occupied by the Venetians and thereby eliminated the danger of a surprise attack on Istanbul. Rebellious soldiers were stricken from the muster rolls and numerous members of the subject class who had been appointed to public office were transferred back to their old positions. This action necessitated mass killings, especially of insurgent cavalrymen. When Mehmed Köprülü died in 1661, however, the mutinies had ceased for the time being.

Köprülü's son Fazıl Ahmed, who was named his father's successor and remained in office until his death in 1676, was by training a teacher of religious law and theology. This background, unusual for a vizier, leads us to assume that he had originally aspired to become a judge. Fazıl Ahmed Köprülü was also quite successful in most of his military enterprises, notably when the Ottoman armies succeeded in restoring the sultan's hegemony in Transylvania. A campaign against the Habsburgs ended with the Treaty of Vasvar (1665), which was quite favorable to the Ottomans despite a severe defeat against the troops commanded by Montecuccoli; the Habsburg emperor had serious concerns on his western frontier, where the "Sun King" Louis XIV had embarked on a career of conquest. Moreover, with the capture of Kandia (Heraklion) in 1669, Fazıl Ahmed Paşa succeeded in completing the Ottoman conquest of Crete after decades of warfare. A series of campaigns in Poland and Lithuania brought the Ottoman Empire to its maximal expansion with the capture of Kamenets-Podolsk in 1672. While several other members of the Köprülü family who also advanced to high offices in the following years did not enjoy the great political fortune of Mehmed and Fazıl Ahmed Paşa, their influence on Sultan Mehmed IV, who was relatively inactive in political matters, assured two decades marked by continuity, political neutrality on the part of the soldiers, and successes in both foreign policy and the military realm.

Changes on the Domestic Front
(from the Late 17th Century to 1774)

With the exceptions of Murad IV and Mustafa II (1695-1703), 17th-century sultans played no outstanding role; as far as the 18th century is concerned only Ahmed III (1703-30) and Selim III (1789-1807) have aroused interest among scholars today. Under the vizierate of the two Köprülüs, the office of grand vizier was enhanced, as we have seen. There were also several strong personalities who served as grand viziers in the 18th century, in particular İbrahim Paşa, often referred to as Nevşehirli İbrahim Paşa (Nevşehir being the city he founded on the site of this natal village) to distinguish him from another grand vizier with the same name.

A distinctly new development was the strong position of other members of the Ottoman bureaucracy, especially of the 'secretary of state' (*reisülküttâb* or *reis efendi*). He was a member of the grand vizier's staff, and his jurisdiction included correspondence with foreign dignitaries. With the increasing significance of diplomatic relations with European states in the 18th century, this office was greatly enhanced. Back in the 16th century, former envoys to European courts rarely attained a high rank in their later careers, but by the second half of the 18th century, such people often had special opportunities for advancement, based on their knowledge of foreign courts. This phenomenon, which would be formative in the Ottoman bureaucracy after about 1840, can thus be regarded as a continuation of older trends.

Other office-holders also achieved an impressive political career: thus Mustafa II appointed his former teacher Feyzullah Efendi as *şeyhülislam* and thereby made him the head of the Ottoman legal and religious scholars. Taking a close interest in military matters, Feyzullah Efendi was also in a position to make decisions concerning the conduct of the Ottoman-Habsburg war, a situation which resulted in protests by the soldiers. However, by taking an active political role, the *şeyhülislam* also lost the protection from corporal punishment that Ottoman *ulema* normally enjoyed: in the rebellion of 1703, Feyzullah and his eldest son were killed while the sultan lost his throne.

In the Ottoman Empire of the 17th and 18th centuries, the ruler thus receded into the background and various office-holders achieved increased power and visibility. Older research tended to consider this development a symptom of Ottoman decline. Scholars today are less inclined to subscribe to this idea: it is useful to recall Max Weber's remark that bureaucratization and routinization typify the modern exercise of power. Overall the Ottoman elite had created stable institutions. Viziers and governors recruited trainees for the state machinery, but the bureaucracy also developed its own dynamic. It can certainly be considered a sign of strength that the Ottoman polity was now able to function without an active sultan if the need arose.

In the provinces, by contrast, the governors who had earlier been appointed by the central administration lost their importance vis-à-vis local tax farmers, who were able to extend their contracts for life after 1695. In the 18th century there were governor dynasties in many places, such as the Jalilis in Mosul and the 'Azms in Damascus, who ruled "their" territories more or less autonomously. In the past, researchers considered this phenomenon a mark of the beginning of 20th-century nation-states, an interpretation that is being rejected by more recent historians. Today we emphasize the considerable Ottoman loyalty of these provincial magnates, which is not to say that they did not pursue their own agendas, for instance in their dealings with the European merchants conducting trade on their territories. The result was an incipient and rather uneven integration of the Ottoman territories into the new capitalist world economy.

War and Peace at the Iranian Border

In 1590, the Shah of Iran, Abbas I (1587-1629), who was still quite young, negotiated a peace agreement with the Ottomans that was favorable for the latter. The sultan gained Azerbaijan, hegemony in the Caucasus, which was previously regarded as an Iranian sphere of influence, and considerable prestige. However, in the following years, Shah Abbas consolidated his rule in the territories that remained under his control and created an army of Georgian slaves, comparable to the janissaries. In 1603/04, Shah Abbas attacked once again and reconquered not only Azerbaijan, but also the important fortress of

Revan (today Erivan in Armenia). An additional campaign led into Iraq, which had been an Ottoman province for nearly a century, and resulted in the conquest of Baghdad. Diyarbakir, the political and commercial center of southern Anatolia, was also captured by Safavid troops in 1623/24. In 1635, however, Sultan Murad IV (1623-40) regained territory taken by Shah Abbas, who had died by this point, in a campaign he personally commanded. These reconquests included Revan and Baghdad. In honor of these two successes, Murad IV had two elegant kiosks built in the garden of the Topkapı palace; they are still standing today. The Treaty of Zuhab or Kasr-i Shirin (1639), which brought several decades of peace, confirmed the Ottoman reconquest of Baghdad.

A new Ottoman-Iranian war was not waged until 1726, this time by Sultan Ahmed III (1703-30), when the Safavid dynasty was drawing to a close and a campaign of Tsar Peter I in the Caucasus had made the weakness of the Iranian defenses manifest. But the Ottoman conquests, including Tabriz, were soon taken back by the Afghan commander Nadir Khan (later Nadir Shah). When a peace treaty was signed in 1730, and again after an additional war in 1746, the border that the two sides agreed upon was based on the old treaty of 1639.

Last Wars against Venice; the Conflict with the Habsburgs

After the loss of Cyprus (1571-73), Venice had little remaining of its colonial empire, which had been in existence since the Late Middle Ages. There were now only a few harbors on the Dalmatian coast, some islands in the Ionian Sea, and the much larger island of Crete, which governed the sea route between Istanbul and Egypt. This latter province continued to play a key role in supplying Istanbul with food, as it had done in late antiquity. The weakened situation of Venice in the 17th century must have prompted the Ottoman campaign of conquest, which dragged on from 1644 to 1669, until, as we have seen, the Köprülüs completed the takeover. When the loss of Crete began to loom on the horizon, the Venetians tried to find a substitute in what is today Greece, especially on the Peloponnesus; in the course of these battles an explosion destroyed the Parthenon in 1687. But in 1715, when these attempts had clearly failed, Venice had to confine its ambitions to its function as a northern Italian regional port, art center, and travel destination for European nobility. Clearly the shift of European long-distance trade routes to the Atlantic and to the Indian Ocean, coupled with the crisis in the German hinterland of Venice during the Thirty Years' War (1618-1648), played an important role in the decline of this commerce-based republic. But it is important to keep in mind the simple fact that the Venetian colonial empire was now essentially in Ottoman hands.

The so-called Long War for control of Hungary was waged with the Habsburgs between 1593 and 1606 (Treaty of Zsitva Torok). Despite a significant Ottoman victory at Mezökeresztes/Haçova in 1596, the sultan's gains were modest, limited to a few Hungarian fortifications. Until 1663, there was a period of peace at the Ottoman-Habsburg border. The sultans stayed out of the Thirty Years' War and the English Civil Wars, which ended with the execution of Charles I in 1649. In the former conflict, the Calvinist king of Bohemia, Frederick V, had tried to win support from the sultans before his defeat in the battle of the White Mountain in 1620; in the latter, Charles sought Ottoman backing before his demise.

New Ottoman advances on Habsburg territory did not occur until the 1660s; a defeat of the Ottoman troops at St. Gotthard on the Raab in 1664 resulted in a nearly twenty-year hiatus from war. In 1683 a new Ottoman campaign led to the famous second siege of Vienna. Top-level Ottoman dignitaries made serious diplomatic and strategic missteps in preparing for this action. When planning its campaign, the Ottoman court had evidently not been informed that the Polish king, Jan Sobieski, who originally had been elected as the representative of the "French" party in the Polish parliament (Sejm), had changed sides after his enthronement and established good relations with the Habsburgs. Or if the relevant information reached Istanbul on time it evidently had not been taken seriously. Ottoman misjudgment of the situation led the Grand Vizier Kara Mustafa Paşa to overlook the possibility of a Polish-Habsburg relief army providing help for the besieged city.

The failure of the Vienna siege in 1683 was a far more serious setback for the Ottomans than the withdrawal had been in 1529, because this time the Habsburgs were able to pursue the retreating Ottoman troops over the border into Hungary. In 1686, the fortress of Buda fell; part of today's Budapest, Buda had been the capital of Ottoman Hungary for about 150 years. The Habsburg troops and their allies occupied a territory the size of the kingdom of Hungary in the Late Middle Ages, including, at least for a brief time, the city and fortress of Belgrade. Transylvania now lost its independence and became a Habsburg territory as well.

Poland, the Russian Empire, the Tatars, and the Cossacks

Already in the second half of the 16th century, Ottoman sultans showed a pronounced interest in the occupants of the Polish royal throne; given that the king was elected by the nobility, it was the major concern to prevent any of the Habsburgs or a prince close to this dynasty from becoming king. Between Poland-Lithuania and the Ottoman state there was a sparsely populated border zone in which the Tatar princes of Crimea waged constant battles with the Cossacks loyal to Poland-Lithuania or to the Russian tsar.

The Cossacks comprised quite diverse groups; in the early period those who recognized the sovereignty of the tsar were often Tatar princes who had lost out in succession battles in their own polity. But a good number of Cossacks were country dwellers who wanted to escape the serfdom that was spreading in Poland and Russia. They spent the summer season hunting and fishing in the estuaries of the Dnjepr and Dnjestr. The Polish aristocracy regarded the Cossacks as a political threat, because they violated the principle of rural serfdom. In the course of the 17th century, their numbers were increasingly restricted by the administration.

For many Cossacks at the beginning of the 17th century, piracy on the Black Sea became a source of income and way of life. They crossed the water on small flat boats, and repeatedly pillaged both Anatolian coastal towns and the area around Istanbul. The difficulty in fighting the pirates was undoubtedly one of the factors that caused the sultans to try to gain control of the borderland inhabited by the Cossacks, which was traversed by major rivers, namely the Prut, Djnestr, Bug, and Dnjepr. The most important Ottoman border fortification was Hotin on the Dnjestr, which was often under attack. After long battles between the three rulers with claims in these areas, which dragged on throughout the 17th century, the borderland was mostly deserted; and the Treaty of Radzin (1681) established the no man's land as an internationally recognized separation zone.

The Tatars formed a principality that was subject to the sultan, the last remnant of the Golden Horde, which had ruled all of Russia in the 13th and 14th centuries. In accordance with standard practice for dependent principalities, the khan was appointed by the Ottoman government, but had to be a member of the ruling family, which regarded itself as descendants of Genghis Khan. In the Ottoman view, this family was the noblest in the empire, just after the sultan's. In times of war, the Tatars formed part of the Ottoman force, but often acted independently of the sultan. Their quick campaigns enabled them several times to burn down Moscow or at least the city's suburbs. Only as part of the Treaty of Radzin (1681) did the sultans promise that forays of this kind would not recur in the future. But enforcing this promise was often a problem, and in the second half of the 18th century, the Ottoman statesman and historian Ahmed Resmi stated baldly that the Tatars were the major cause of wars between sultans and tsars.

The expeditions of Tsar Peter I against the Ottomans did not result in lasting Russian conquests, but when the tsar appeared on the border, Demetrius Cantemir, the scholarly prince of Moldavia and a vassal of the sultan, was easily persuaded to switch sides. To preclude a repetition of this kind of betrayal in the future, the practice of nominating local personages as princes of Moldavia and Wallachia, both located in today's Romania, was henceforth given up. From the early 1700s governors from prominent Greek families of Istanbul, the so-called Phanariots, took the place of locally-based dynasties.

The effects of the Russian-Ottoman War of 1768-74 were more serious and lasting than those of the conflict with Peter I. The sultan had become embroiled in this war to contain the influence of the tsar in Poland and to win back Podolia, which had been lost in 1699. A Russian fleet sailed from the Baltic Sea to the eastern Mediterranean in 1770 and destroyed the Ottoman warships near Çeşme. The commanders of the Tsarina Catherine II also ignited a revolt on the Peloponnesus, which was crushed by the Ottoman vizier Muhsinzade Mehmed Paşa. But the Albanian irregular troops recruited during this campaign were not paid, and in reprisal, they soon terrorized the inhabitants of the peninsula to the point that an additional Ottoman campaign was necessary to dislodge them from their positions. The long-term bitterness that these anarchic wars aroused helped set the stage for the Greek revolution of 1821. The Treaty of Küçük Kaynarca (1774), which finally ended the war after several unsuccessful attempts at peace-making, resulted in severe losses for the Ottoman Empire. Crimea was the first Muslim territory to be lost; it was finally annexed by the Russians in 1783. Equally critical was the fact that the Black Sea, which had been an Ottoman lake closed to foreign ships for about three centuries, now had to be opened to European navigation.

Succession to the Throne and Dynastic Self-Representation

Until quite recently, historians have used the expression "sultanate of women" in describing the late 16th and the first half of the 17th century, when the mothers of the sultans (Valide Sultan) played an important political role. Contemporaries tended to react quite negatively to the great power of these women. But a feminist approach in historiography has made us aware of just how widespread misogyny "on principle" was, not only among the Ottomans, but also in

Europe. Consequently, historians today are less inclined to take accusations against the sultans' mothers at face value.

When the rulers were themselves underage, their mothers had reason to become active; and both Murad IV and Mehmed IV (1648-87) acceded to the throne as small children. It is by no means certain that the sultans' mothers in this period were really as inexperienced in political matters as is often claimed; after all, the harem was a complex, sophisticated, and exceedingly hierarchical institution, and those who rose within this context acquired considerable political skill.[1]

New research has shown that the importance of the sultans' mothers in the life of the dynasty shifted when the system of succession changed. Until the mid-16th century, it had been standard practice for a concubine who had borne the sultan a son to move to the provinces with her offspring as soon as the prince was old enough to assume a governorship – albeit with a tutor in the background.[2] But when Suleiman the Magnificent, Kanuni in Turkish parlance, married Hürrem (Roxelane), their relationship was so close that most of the sons of this ruler competing for the throne had the same mother. In the disputes between her sons, Hürrem Sultan's hands were tied. But when it came to Sultan Suleiman's sons from earlier unions, Hürrem Sultan "went by the book" when she took action against her stepsons and promoted her own descendants as best she could. The only difference was that these maneuvers no longer took place in the seclusion of a provincial palace, but in full view of the court in Istanbul. This situation probably explains why Hürrem Sultan was regarded as a schemer exceeding her proper limits, especially by those who wanted to see a prince from one of Suleiman's earlier unions accede to the throne.

The princes' mothers of the following generations, toward the end of the 16th century, encountered an altogether different situation, because the regulations governing succession that had been in effect since the reign of Mehmed the Conqueror were once again in flux. Selim's successor, Murad III, was the last to have been educated in the provinces. From then on, princes remained in the palace, under the watchful eye of the ruler, and nearly devoid of contact with the outside world. By the 17th century, the rule that the sultan have his brothers killed when acceding to the throne was implemented far less often and finally lapsed. Instead, an institutionalized succession to the throne was developed in which the oldest member of the House of Osman acceded to the throne.

As a consequence, a prince's mother no longer left the sultan's palace for the provinces. By remaining in Istanbul, these women had opportunities to wield political influence right in the center of power. Besides taking part in palace intrigues, they could cultivate connections with janissaries stationed in the capital. The elaborate pious foundations that some sultans' mothers established are evidence of their power, although the buildings they constructed generally bore only the title of the donor (Valide Sultan) rather than her personal name. The status of the sultans' mothers at this time was even enhanced when the ruler relocated his royal residence to the harem in the second half of the 16th century. Because his mother was in charge of this institution, the monarch thus spent a good deal of his time in the Valide Sultan's territory.

In the mid-17th century, under the pressure of wars abroad and crises at home, a reform of government structures took place, which granted the grand vizier a great deal of power and severely restricted that of the palace women. But by the 18th century, the female members of the sultan's family were again playing a visible role. Rather than the mothers, however, it was now the daughters and sisters of reigning sultans who occupied center stage. These young women were given palaces at the Bosporus when they married high dignitaries. They had an important role in shaping the image of the sultan's family until a "neo-absolutist" sultan's regime was installed in the 19th century, which limited their influence once again.

Scholars, Travelers, and Political Writers[3]

In the 17th century, the Ottoman capital developed an active and multifaceted intellectual life despite all its domestic and foreign crises.

Kâtib Çelebi ("the scribe" and "the gentleman"; real name: Mustafa bin Abdullah, 1609-57; also called Haji Khalifa in European sources) produced a major bibliography of Islamic works that is still used today, as well as a chronicle and writings on state reforms. But the most famous of his numerous works was likely his book on geography, "View of the World" (*Cihân-numâ*), which set out not only to summarize geographical knowledge about the Ottoman provinces, but also to incorporate this knowledge into the categories that he had discovered in translations of Dutch atlases, especially the *Atlas minor*. The author rewrote his work several times, integrating the findings of new publications he had come across. At his death it was still unfinished, and had to be completed by his friends. The book was published in 1732, as one of the first Ottoman works to appear in print.[4]

Kâtib Çelebi's contemporary Evliya Çelebi (ca. 1610-1685) was less scholarly, but most original. Evliya had been educated at the palace, but he kept rejecting offers of influential posts, preferring instead to travel throughout the Ottoman Empire, as well as to several areas near the border, such as the Sudan, West Iran, and Vienna.[5] Evliya knew the geographical literature of both the medieval Arabic and the Ottoman traditions, but giving an exact account of them and revising them where necessary, the way a scholar would have approached the project, was not his intention. Instead, he made his knowledge and experiences the basic framework of a travel narrative, a genre that was previously unfamiliar in Ottoman literature and which disappointed readers who wanted to use Evliya's work as a geographical source. But for readers who accept the fictional element, the travel narrative is exciting and instructive to read.

Kâtib Çelebi and Evliya Çelebi were Ottomans by birth, but several notable new arrivals from Europe who converted to Islam also bear mention. Ali Ufki (ca. 1610-1675) was originally Polish; his Latinized name had been Albertus Bobovius. For a long time he directed the choir of the pages in Topkapı Sarayı. Because of the high value that was placed on music in palace culture, this activity carried a great deal of responsibility. He used the musical knowledge he evidently had acquired in Poland to record the notes sung by the choir of pages.

Many of his musical notations have been preserved. Ali Ufki's intellectual life seems to have kept oscillating between the Ottoman-Islamic and the European-Christian worlds. He spent his entire later life in Istanbul and made friends there with learned Ottomans, as well as with Antoine Galland (1646-1715), the translator of the *Thousand and One Nights* into French, who also lived in the Ottoman capital for a long time. Most of his works are now in European libraries, but during his lifetime, Ali Ufki's knowledge was beneficial primarily to the pupils in the palace school, whom he tutored in singing.[6]

In the 17th and 18th centuries, there were also notable Ottoman historiographers. Mustafa Naima (1655-1716) came from the northern Syrian city of Aleppo and thus spoke Arabic as well as Ottoman-Turkish. His major historical work covers an epoch that he did not experience as an eyewitness (1591-1660), as is often the case in this genre. An introduction contains Naima's thoughts on history and politics. His argument is based on the social theories of the Northern African scholar Ibn Khaldun (1332-82), who felt that a high degree of social solidarity makes it relatively easy for inhabitants of the steppe and desert to found states. But after settling in, this solidarity invariably dissolves and the states in question undergo stages of development analogous to those normally attributed to living beings. Ibn Khaldun's ideas had a pronounced impact on members of the sultan's inner circle who wrote analyses of the situation in the Ottoman state. In his Ottoman chronicle, Naima discussed by what ways and means it could be possible to prolong the life of the sultanate while accepting that in Ibn Khaldun's terms it had passed its prime.

Ahmed Resmi (1700-83) is notable among the historians and political writers of the 18th century because of his own long political and diplomatic experience. His travel reports as an ambassador to Berlin amusingly describe the curiosity of the residents in the Prussian capital, who had never seen a real Turk before.[7] But Ahmed Resmi had the most significant experiences of his life during the Russian-Ottoman War of 1768-1774. Resmi had warned against this venture, but was unable to prevail over the pro-war party. He concluded that Muslim and non-Muslim states were subject to the same political rules, the most important of which entailed the suitability of ends and means. A ruler who overestimated the "natural opportunities" available to his empire would only weigh down his subjects with excessive taxes.

The Ottoman View of Europe and the Enhancement of Local Traditions

It would be a gross oversimplification to assume that there was no cultural contact between the Ottoman Empire and Europe before the 18th century. There certainly was contact—however sporadic—in the realm of courtly art once Mehmed the Conqueror had invited the Venetian painter Gentile Bellini to Istanbul. When Evliya Çelebi visited Vienna in 1665, he was particularly impressed by the organ in the St. Stephen's Cathedral, and he also admired the architecture of the St. Stephen's Tower and the skill of Viennese surgeons. He pointed out the error of the assumption that Christians worshipped images; these images, he explained, were actually used as pedagogical tools (*Biblia pauperum* [Paupers' Bible]).[8] We can only speculate how he came up with this information.

In the 18th century, Ottoman courtly contacts with Europe, especially with France, increased substantially. A first attempt occurred during the reign of Sultan Ahmed III (1703-30), who dispatched an ambassador to provide a detailed report on life at the court of the young Louis XV and on the highlights of Paris. The report of this Ottoman ambassador, named Yirmisekiz Mehmed Çelebi, is full of sharp-eyed observations.[9] Selected on the basis of his ability to interact with people, he traveled with his son, who soon struck up a friendship with young French noblemen, who provided yet another source of valuable social contacts.

Ottoman interest in European art is apparent in the courtly art of miniature painting. This art was shaped by Levni, a miniaturist who was commissioned by Ahmed III to provide a series of illustrations commemorating the circumcision ceremonies for Ahmed's sons in

1720. But he also produced elegant individual sheets portraying young people in various kinds of traditional dress, including European clothing. Levni and his students experimented with themes that posed new artistic challenges. Abdullah Buhari depicted a young woman bathing, while an anonymous painter in the same circle sought to recreate festive fireworks, and produced the first Ottoman representation of a night sky.

The fashion of decorating elegant houses and mosques with pictures of landscapes was also remarkable in this context. At the beginning of the 18th century, there was a quest in courtly circles to find alternatives to the customary flowers and ornaments without violating the Islamic law forbidding representations of people and animals. Urban vedute were especially popular. Local dignitaries in the provinces were quite fond of pictures of the capital with its mosques, boats, and islands. These pictures were essentially derived from miniatures in manuscript illuminations, but there were also experiments with light and shadow and the recreation of three-dimensional space. Unfortunately we have no information as to the identity of the painters and their work methods.

Ottoman interest in European art was only one form of the quest for new inspirations in the art of the 18th century. Egyptians looked to Mamluk models; an innovative patron, such as Abd al-Rahman Katkhoda (ca. 1714-76), could even inspire a new style. The family of İshak Paşa, whose power basis was the town of Doğubeyazit at the Ottoman-Iranian border, took a highly unconventional approach when having their palace built in the second half of the 18th century. The palace was clearly based on Seljuk architecture, which had had its heyday a good five hundred years earlier.

Life in the Country

After the 16th century, central registers of Ottoman taxpayers were no longer compiled, and we have to rely on local or regional sources for this information. It is therefore difficult to make supraregional comparisons. We have already discussed the civil wars of the period around 1600, which resulted in a considerable loss of population in central Anatolia and elsewhere. In some parts of Anatolia, taxes could no longer be collected because the peasants had fled; sometimes they settled in remote areas that appeared to offer better protection. The Ottoman office-holders thus located villagers from the eastern portion of central Anatolia in the extreme western part of the peninsula, right next to the capital. In other cases, the peasants who remained built refuges in which they barricaded themselves to avoid robbers and fugitive soldiers—and the tax collector.

In a clear overestimation of his own success at establishing peace, Sultan Murad IV (1623-40) tried to make the refugees return to their former provinces. In reality, that was possible only in isolated instances, because often the peasants had sold their property before fleeing, or it had been occupied by others. Frequently these usurpers were people who had used their influence in the Ottoman state to get estates. The forests and steppes did not offer much in the way of security either, as is evident from a fascinating report by Grigor, an Armenian priest from the eastern Anatolian town of Kemah, who had to return to his home with a caravan of Muslims and Christians by order of Murad IV. It was a true odyssey.[10] Thus the unrest in the period around 1600 had a lasting impact on patterns of settlement, at least in Anatolia. While the well-situated areas around the harbor city of Izmir that began to prosper in the 17th century probably recorded an increase in population, the villages of the Central Anatolian steppe often diminished in size or even disappeared. Only in the hill country, on inaccessible islands in rivers and moors, and in the better-protected areas near major towns could many villages remain intact.

During the 16th century, numerous western and central Anatolian nomads had settled down more or less permanently, but new tribal groups from the eastern part of the country immigrated after 1600, apparently attracted by the open areas between the settlements. It is reasonably easy to trace the advance of one group of this kind. After a stop along the way west of Konya, it eventually showed up on the island of Rhodes. The peasants often complained about these newcomers, who owned horses and weapons and thus were militarily superior to the villagers unless the state intervened. Camels or sheep were often driven into the fields before they had been harvested, and into the gardens as well, which was at least as damaging. While there were also peaceful relations between villagers and nomads, these complaints were taken very seriously by the Ottoman central government.

Farmers were easier to tax than tribal groups, so the Ottoman government began systematic attempts to settle nomads toward the end of the 17th century. The border area between present-day Syria and Turkey was taken into consideration as the land for development; the Ottoman office-holders evidently hoped that the new settlers would maintain their military potential for a while and defend themselves and their neighbors against attacks by desert nomads. But in the end, the tribal groups were allotted land that was not very suitable for farming. Although the Ottoman administration had sent specialists ahead to figure out where wells could be dug, it is far from certain that their recommendations were followed. Also, the new settlers were not given any means to tide them over during the first difficult years in their new way of life, so many of them soon gave up their residences again, and because they had lost a large portion of their livestock, they had little choice but to resort to robbery.[11]

Village-style farming and cattle breeding by tribal groups were at first meant for personal use, although a portion of this production was also put on the market. In some areas, however, agricultural products were intended chiefly for sale. Olives were grown in northern Syria, in the region around Jerusalem, in the vicinity of the northwestern Anatolian district of Edremit, and above all in Tunisia and on the island of Crete, which was conquered by the Ottomans in 1645-69. Olive oil did not have the dominant place in the Ottoman diet that it holds in today's Turkish cuisine. For this reason, the oil was used either for illumination—olive oil was sent as far as Mecca and Medina for use in mosque lamps—or to make soap. Northern Syria, the area surrounding Jerusalem, and Crete were known for their soap making. Significant amounts of olive oil were exported from Crete, Tunisia, and the Peloponnesus to Marseilles, where it was also used for soap making. In the coastal area of Tunisia, the export of olives resulted in a close tie to the southern French economy in the 18th century, that is, to a regional "incorporation."

The cultivation of cotton was also often market-oriented. This plant had a long tradition in the coastal plains of the eastern Mediterranean; because of the importance of cotton in the production of sailcloth, the Ottoman authorities often forbade the export of this product in the 16th century. But this practice changed after about 1600, and by the 18th century, cotton, both raw and spun and dyed, was one of the Empire's important exports, and drew merchants from Marseilles to Izmir or to Sayda in Southern Syria. The cultivation seems to have been left to small farmers rather than being undertaken by plantation owners. The local tax collectors had an important role only in marketing, and some were able to earn enough money to become local magnates.

Ottoman and European Economy

Between about 1720 and 1765, business and trade experienced a period of expansion in many centers of the Ottoman Empire. In the Balkans, mule drivers sometimes became shippers or businessmen who specialized in long-distance trade; in these capacities, they attended the Leipzig Fair. The first step in this direction was for the mule drivers to take along products made during the winter at home to sell them in the spring at markets far from home. This is how the weaving of coarse and sturdy wool fabrics developed in present-day southern Bulgaria, in the area of Plovdiv. The local merchants were able to increase their sales quite substantially by using strategies we would today describe as aggressive marketing.

There were signs of economic expansion in other parts of the Ottoman Empire as well. In the Ottoman port cities, European merchants were feeling stiff competition from local Christian merchants. Cotton print fabrics and copper goods were also produced in the inland Anatolian city of Tokat, while cotton and light silk fabrics were woven in Bursa. The manufacture of silk also flourished on the island of Chios. In present-day southeastern Anatolia and northern Syria, the manufacturers of cotton prints sought to attract customers who had been buying imports from India since the 17th century. Skillful copies of Indian fabrics from these eastern Mediterranean centers were at times even exported to France.

We can only speculate as to the reasons for this expansion and why it came to an end between 1760 and 1770. It appears significant that only brief periods of war punctuated the decades after the Treaty of Pasarofça in 1718, at least at the western and northern fronts, and the Ottoman state undertook serious efforts to make the trade routes safe again for merchants. Fortified stopping points for caravans were built, and they sometimes developed into small urban centers. These measures were attempts to reverse the damage caused by the wars in 1683-99, when the concentration of all resources in the Balkans had led to the uncontrolled spread of robbers on the roads of Anatolia and Syria.

It is also of some interest that in France, the economy expanded during the mid-eighteenth century; in other words during approximately the same years as the flourishing of Ottoman trade and manufactures. This convergence might indicate an integration of the Ottoman Empire as a whole into the "world economy" dominated by Europe. If so, this integration must have occurred earlier than is assumed by most experts today, namely in the 17th century or possibly even in the late 16th. However, this parallel growth may be more or less coincidental; and many historians today consider the closing decades of the 18th century as well as the first quarter of the 19th the crucial period of change. Exporting craft products was of moderate importance to Ottoman and foreign traders during the 1700s; and the work of local craftsmen typically went to the Ottoman domestic market. Quite possibly developments outside the empire's borders were still of limited importance for the fate of its industries.

But after about 1750, the world economic integration of coastal regions, such as the area around the Aegean, seems to have progressed rapidly. This process did not always go hand in hand with a decline in local industrial production, even though that was often the case. Thus in the late 1700s merchants and spinners in the small Thessalonian town of Ambelakia supplied Austrian and Bohemian workshops with high-quality cotton thread; and some local merchants profited substantially. But when hand-spun yarn was no longer in demand the industry rapidly declined; as this example shows, Ottoman producers and merchants were now at the mercy of fluctuations in demand in very remote economic centers, where they did not have the least bit of control.

There has been some reflection as to why the wars in the late 18th century did not lead to an economic boom in the armaments sector, but rather to a crisis in which weapons manufacturers and food purveyors were no longer able to provide adequate supplies to the Ottoman armies. It has been suggested that the financing methods of the Ottoman central administration were the root cause of this problem, because it was common to pay the producers of these war supplies far less than their production costs, or even to demand these supplies for free. The result was a lack of capital and long-term economic weakness. But why had similar methods had better outcomes in the 16th and 17th centuries? Part of the reason appears to be that waging war in the early modern age was becoming more and more costly. Without a corresponding economic expansion no capital could be accumulated; and as a result it became impossible to satisfactorily supply the sultans' armies. The limits placed on the accumulation of capital had been a perennial weak point in the Ottoman economy; given rising costs, by the later 1700s the empire no longer could mobilize the resources needed for modern war.

Ottoman Women

There are more locally oriented sources available on the subject of urban women outside the realm of palace circles after about 1600 than for older periods. Many of these sources revolved around questions pertaining to the assets held by women. Islamic religious law granted the right to inherit—albeit only half the share that would have been accorded to a man of the same degree of relationship. Still more significant was the fact that a married woman was able to control her assets on her own, had legal capacity, and was entitled to file suit in court, even against her husband. Many women complained that their male relatives were trying to force them out of their share of the inheritance. The archives of the *kadı* offices often list unpaid debts as well, because many urban women earned a modest income by lending money. Albeit to a lesser extent women also owned houses and gardens.

Our sources thus reflect the problems facing women who had some money to their names. The very poorest women—and men—were rarely documented. Still, we learn that in Ankara in the period around 1600, families without resources were known to press their small daughters into service as maids (*besleme*). Other texts record women who were freed from slavery and received a dowry. There are also reports of spinners who worked for merchants. Textile centers such as Bursa and Ankara seem to have offered women greater opportunities to earn money working at home.

The activities of well-to-do women were most likely to be recorded when they established a pious foundation. Existing family foundations could be expanded, and freed slavewomen could be supported when a foundation belonging to a woman who had owned them gave them a roof over their head. Foundations to benefit mosques were common, but at least in 18th-century Bursa, women were also known to take care of street and bridge repair.

An area of additional research interest is the religious, artistic, and literary activity of women. In theory, prepubescent girls could attend a Koran school, but most women who learned how to read and write were instructed at home. Particularly in families of religious and legal scholars, and of dervishes, women could typically read and write. As far as "official" religious doctrine, they were granted the authority to transmit sayings of the prophet (*hadis*), in accordance with early Islamic traditions. The letters a female dervish from the Macedonian city of Üsküb (today: Skopje) wrote to her sheikhs in the 17th century have been preserved. The fact that her family kept the drafts of her letters is evidence of the esteem they felt for her.

There were also occasional female voices in Ottoman poetry. In 18th-century Istanbul, Fitnet Hatun made a name for herself in this field; her assertiveness seems to have intimidated her male colleagues. Nothing is known about works by the fairly numerous female musicians in pre-19th-century upper-class houses. In the fine arts, there were embroiderers and carpet weavers, but before the 19th century, works of this kind were rarely signed. Still, recent findings suggest that new discoveries may be forthcoming.[12]

CHAPTER 4

◆ ◆ ◆

"The Longest Century of the Empire"[1]

(From Küçük Kaynarca to the End of World War I)

Political and Military Crises
at the Turn of the Nineteenth Century

The crushing defeats in the wars of 1768-74 led the Ottoman political establishment to focus squarely on the introduction of European military technology, especially after Sultan Selim III's accession to the throne (1789-1807). These efforts were continued throughout the 19th century, but even so, few wars ended successfully for the Ottomans. The reasons are more likely economic and political than military in the narrower sense. Until the end of the 18th century, the majority of Ottoman subjects, including the Christians in the Balkans, had not been inclined to obey conspirators' calls to action against Ottoman rule, although there were plenty of these calls, particularly in the 16th century. That changed in the 19th century, when the idea of nationalism, with or without religious overtones, mobilized the provincial elites, and soon thereafter the "ordinary" subjects as well.

Moreover, by 1800, the opponents of the Ottoman Empire had gained novel resources that allowed them to engage in power politics on a scale unimaginable two centuries earlier. England had made great strides on the path to industrialization and acquired a great number of colonial possessions in India, the defense of which required active involvement in the Mediterranean region. Napoleon did not succeed in acquiring Egypt as a colony for France, but Algeria was conquered in 1830, and in 1881 Tunisia became a French possession. Moreover, during the late 17th and early 18th centuries the Habsburg monarchy had made major advances into the Balkans. But the most dangerous enemy for the Ottoman state was without a doubt tsarist Russia. For one thing, the tsars laid claim to a kind of protectorate over the Orthodox Christians of the Balkans; for another, the Russian rulers had built up important military power since the early 18th century.

If one adds to these political factors the "incorporation" into the world economy, dominated by Europe, that had been taking place rapidly since the end of the 18th century, it is clear that especially after about 1815 the Ottoman Empire was in an extremely precarious position.

Despite the sultans' interest in initiating structural changes in the military in the early 19th century, opportunities for innovation in this area were severely restricted, at least until 1826. The new technologies required specially trained soldiers, but these soldiers would have competed with the janissaries, who had close ties to the craftsmen in the big cities, as we saw earlier. But the craftsmen's ability to eke out a living depended on the tax privileges they enjoyed because of their membership in the military corps, which had evolved into militias. This limited economic leeway also explains why the janissaries adamantly opposed all innovations that would have compromised their privileges.

Craftsmen doubling as militiamen found support for their position among the less prosperous legal and religious scholars (*ulema*). Those who did not belong to established families and had completed their education in the provinces found that they were forced into less lucrative offices. Under conditions of financial stringency it made sense for these people to link the legitimacy of the state with the fulfillment of religious precepts. The *ulema*, even those in modest positions, thus justified their status as guardians of the Muslim community. If the Muslims lived according to the precepts of Islam, so the argument went, victorious campaigns could not fail to materialize with God's help, and there was no need to copy the habits of the "infidels."

By contrast, members of the Ottoman upper class, such as the aforementioned Ahmed Resmi, had a very pragmatic attitude. In order to emerge victorious once again, they reasoned, they would first have to compensate for previous political and military errors. The result was a demand for strategic and tactical reform. But diplomacy also gained in importance, so as to anticipate the shifting alliances that were so typical of European politics.

An argument advanced by certain Ottoman chroniclers of the late 16th century now reappeared in this context, namely that it would be a serious mistake to assume that God would automatically bring about the victory of the Muslims against the infidels. Ahmed Resmi for instance emphasized that the rules of politics and war apply to all states, and anyone who did not go by these rules was only setting himself up for defeat. This issue gave rise to a conflict of the sort we continue to encounter in diverse forms until 1918 and beyond. A split occurred between many members of the governing classes, which by and large were prepared to experiment with modern technical and institutional imports from Europe in order to preserve the empire, and the lower class, many of whose members considered this route fundamentally wrong. An extreme divergence between the culture of the upper and lower classes emerged at this time, a divergence that would characterize the 19th century as a whole. It goes without saying there had been socio-cultural differences between upper and lower classes in earlier epochs as well, but those differences had never had a bearing on such fundamental issues as the relationship between religion and politics. The fact that the Ottoman upper class did not succeed in holding the empire together in the long run fueled the arguments of those who opposed "Ottoman pragmatism."

Sultan Selim III tried to introduce military reforms by forming a special military corps called the "New Order." European instructors conducted the training, and the soldiers were equipped with better weaponry. But the sultan was deposed and eventually murdered. In view of this threat, when Selim's nephew, Mahmud II (1808-39), acceded to the throne, he spent more than a decade merely consolidating his power. He built a base for himself in the provinces by driving back the notables and magnates who had come to power during the 18th century; those who survived his centralizing drive settled for non-political landownership or else went into the service of the central administration.

This policy was largely successful in the central provinces. Then the sultan again created a modernized military. The janissaries rebelled and suffered a devastating defeat, and the military corps was dismantled. Now the lower *ulema* had lost their strongest social support, and urban revolts of the kind that had been frequent in the 18th century were virtually out of the question. Sultan Mahmud II thus established a neo-absolutist regime of a sort that had been absolutely unknown to his predecessors in the 17th and 18th centuries.

Egypt and the European Great Powers

Mahmud II was adhering to patterns of behavior that had previously been practiced by Mehmed Ali (Muhammad Ali), his governor in Egypt. From the Ottoman conquest of 1517 to the early 19th century, this province had been governed by freed military slaves (Mamluks). While Mamluks had controlled Egpyt since the 13th century, the conditions under which they operated came to differ radically once an Ottoman garrison was established in Cairo and they owed an annual tribute to the central government in Istanbul. Since the late 17th century, however, the politically relevant households in which the Mamluks (and many other officers in Cairo) came to be organized had become increasingly autonomous. From Istanbul's perspective, the rule of the Mamluk households had proved counterproductive when their army was defeated by Napoleon in a single battle in 1798. Napoleon's attempt to control Egypt ultimately failed, but the Ottoman reconquest was a long, drawn-out process, despite the support of England, and in 1805, Selim III recognized Mehmed Ali, the second-in-command of this campaign, as governor. Mehmed Ali consolidated his rule by having the heads of the leading Mamluk households and many of their supporters killed in 1807 and putting a stop to the recruitment of new military slaves.

Even in this early phase, however, Mehmed Ali set his sights on more than a typical governorship. Initially his support was crucially important to the new sultan, Mahmud II, since the Egyptian army was the only strong military force available to the Ottoman central government at this time. Egyptian troops quelled the Greek revolution; the fact that a Greek state was founded anyway was a consequence of the interests of the great powers of Europe.

Mehmed Ali's successes resulted from a standing army that was recruited from the Egyptian peasant class. Their provisions were supplied by a system of state-owned factories, which in turn received raw materials from the ruler's trade monopoly. The factories that produced weapons, ammunition, and textiles were able to stay afloat financially as long as the army was a steady purchaser. Between 1830 and 1840, it seemed as though the foundations of industrialization were being created with state capitalist methods in Egypt. A war between Mehmed Ali, who was aiming for autonomous rule in Egypt and Syria, and his Ottoman overlord from 1831 to 1833 did little to impede Egyptian progress. In several battles, the armies of the Egyptian magnate, commanded by his son Ibrahim Paşa, did extremely well.

The sultan ultimately survived by mobilizing the support of the European great powers, especially England. The industrialization of Egypt posed a threat to European, especially British, markets and sources of raw materials. Moreover, many Europeans were dismayed at the notion of an "Oriental" ruler competing for equal power and status, who ought to be "put in his place." In 1840, Mehmed Ali was confronted with the alternative of facing the ordeal of a war against England or returning to the sovereignty of the sultan and giving up the conquered territories, including Syria. The end of Egyptian expansion signified the acknowledgement of the Ottoman customs regime, making it impossible to continue state-sponsored industrialization, which was already in trouble because of the inadequacy of many goods produced by inexperienced factory managers to the requirements of the Egyptian domestic market. Even so, Mehmed Ali's attempt to industrialize a province of the empire largely failed because incorporation into the European economic system had already taken place.

National Movements in the Balkans (1803-1912)

The activities of the Greek merchant fleets laid the economic foundations for the Greek revolution of 1821. In the wars of the revolutionary epoch, such as the Napoleonic era (1792-1815), Greek merchants did not face any competition from the French, who had traditionally been active in this sector, and they exploited this opportunity for powerful expansion and capital accumulation. Control of ships and maritime routes enabled the Greeks to foster key international connections, in particular with the tsars of Russia, who had just acquired new territories in the Black Sea region and were seeking capital and know-how. The Greeks seemed especially suitable partners because they shared an Orthodox creed with the Russians.[2] This "Russian connection" explains why the Greek revolution of 1821 was initiated by an exile organization based in Odessa.

From the perspective of the tsars, the Greek desire to found a state represented a golden opportunity to expand Russian influence to the Balkans. Given the powerful English naval presence in the Mediterranean, it was important for the emerging state to maintain a good relationship with England and to promote English trade. Moreover, the Greek merchants were regarded as creditworthy in Europe, thus enabling the insurgents to finance their war against the Ottoman Empire with loans. In 1830, the European great powers enforced the establishment of a Greek state on the Peloponnesus and in Attica that was independent on paper but was actually under their protectorate. Prince Otto of Bavaria (1833-62) became king for a time.

The beginning of the Serbian revolt dated back to the years around 1800, when the many aggressions of the Belgrade janissary garrison set the population against them. Sultan Selim III, who, as we have seen, was pursuing military reform, initially supported the efforts of his Serbian subjects to contain the janissaries. But the defeat of this sultan on the domestic front turned the Serbian revolt into an uprising against Ottoman rule as a whole. The principality of Serbia had been recognized internationally as a small autonomous entity since 1830, although it was still part of the Ottoman Empire. In Greece, there were two distinct social groups engaged in a degree of political competition: a small, quite wealthy class of merchants at the Mediterranean coast, and poor peasants and herdsmen who plowed barren mountainous fields or tended flocks. The principality of Serbia, by contrast, was an entirely rural society, with the export of livestock as the only "currency earner."

As for present-day Romania, Transylvania was part of the Habsburg Empire in the 19th century. Moldavia and Walachia were Ottoman territories, but these areas were ruled by Christian governors in the name of the sultan. In the course of the 19th century, this local autonomy increased. The social structure also differed fundamentally from the centrally ruled Ottoman provinces. The local nobility ("boyars") established the institution of serfdom, which was otherwise unknown in Ottoman territory.

Because of its geographical position, the territory comprising present-day Bulgaria developed autonomy and independence movements far more slowly than the rest of the Balkans. Dependence on the policies of the Russian Empire was even greater here than in the other Balkan states. As in Greece, a period of economic development preceded the blossoming of the national movement. After 1826, the manufacturers of woolen cloth in the Plovdiv area became suppliers for the Ottoman army. But early industrial production expanded even apart from this new market. Notable cultural endeavors also preceded the political movement. Bulgarian merchants objected to the preeminence of the Greek language in ecclesiastical practice, and the so-called exarchate was established as a church organization independent of the ecumenical patriarch residing in Istanbul. Ottoman policy tolerated this church that competed with the "Greek" one, and for the Bulgarians, affiliation with the exarchate constituted a form of pre-national organization.

All the territories discussed here were rural societies without the kinds of factories and industry that typified the 19th century in western and central Europe and the United States. While in Bulgaria a few factories had been established in the mid-19th century to service the Ottoman military, their economic impact was limited and for the

most part they faded away after the Bulgarian provinces gained a
degree of independence through the Russo-Ottoman War of 1877-78.
This meant that military supplies often had to be imported. In
Greece, Serbia, and Bulgaria, the political landscape was dominated
by groups of politicians who aimed to annex additional areas into the
"motherlands." In many cases irredentism was supported by the local
rulers, who were often members of foreign dynasties and tried to
legitimize their new positions by promoting territorial expansion. No
Balkan state regarded itself as what the diplomatic language of the
19th century might have described as "saturated." Relatively large
armies were maintained, which contributed to a high national debt
and in some cases even to national bankruptcy.

Yet until the 1870s, such campaigns for expansion quite often
failed because they conflicted with British interests; for until this time
British government circles preferred to maintain the Ottoman state as
a bulwark against the expanding tsarist empire.

Until the last quarter of the 19th century, since the territories they
sought to acquire were always Ottoman, the Balkan principalities had
common interests; and only one single Balkan power laid claim to a
given territory. But this changed after about 1870, when rival nation-
states demanded the integration of ethnically mixed or not easily clas-
sifiable areas. Adherents of the so-called Megali Idea ("Great Idea")
in Greece hoped to acquire the entire territory of the former Byzantine Empire, and the Greek government under Venizelos attempted to
achieve this plan after the end of World War I by means of a campaign in western Anatolia. Only the utter failure of this enterprise in
1922 discredited the project.

A point of contention between Bulgaria, Greece, and Serbia was
Macedonia, which was still in Ottoman hands. Since it was assumed
that the future affiliation of the area would essentially be determined
by the self-identification of the inhabitants, each of the three neighboring states had its own school system, with a curriculum tailored to
the propagandistic needs of the particular state. Worse still for the
residents of Macedonia, Bulgarian guerrillas attempted to draw
Macedonians to their side by means of terrorist actions. The frustra-

tion of the Ottoman officers at the prospect of a long guerrilla war—entailing a loss of salary and home leaves—would play a significant role in the revolt against Sultan Abdülhamid in 1908.

Another source of tension was the situation of the Albanians, who by the 19th century had largely become Muslims. Opposition to the Ottomans was here triggered by the military reforms of the period, which involved the disarming of local populations, as well as universal taxation and conscription. Many Albanians had hitherto served in the Ottoman military, often as irregulars, either in the armies of the central government or in those of local magnates. However, those clansmen who had provided soldiers were categorically opposed to conscription and new-style military discipline. In addition, once the Ottoman Empire began to lose territory in the Balkans on a massive scale, educated Albanians started to demand autonomy so as to avoid becoming part of Orthodox national states that often expelled their Muslim subjects.

Enshrined in a document that became known as the Fourteen Points, concrete demands included the concentration of all lands inhabited by Albanians in a single province that was to be administered by officials of local background. Except in wartime, Albanian recruits were to serve only in their home territory; this was an attempted compromise between the central state's demand for conscripts and the insistence of local clans on a volunteer army. In addition, schools in the province were to teach in Albanian. In the early 20th century an Albanian uprising whose leaders put forth these demands was to trigger a series of wars that would end with the collapse of the Ottoman Empire.

There is no need to go into detail here about the wars in which the Ottoman Empire was embroiled between 1803 and 1912. In all cases, the success or failure of the Ottoman troops was only one of the—less important—variables that determined the outcome. What mattered was the attempt on the part of the great powers involved in the Balkans and in the Mediterranean region not to let any rival become too powerful in this strategically important area, which is why the peace treaties focused on provisions on which the great powers in question were able to agree. The government of the sultan had no more than a secondary role in all of this.

Even a list of the military entanglements clearly reveals the burden facing the subjects of the empire. Apart from the Egyptian advances between 1831 and 1833, and again between 1839 and 1841, the Greek revolution lasted throughout the 1820s. In 1828-29 there was a war with tsarist Russia. For a short time, it appeared as though the Ottoman Empire would become a Russian protectorate. In the Crimean War (1853-56), the sultan was on the side of the victors, but that had no long-term consequences. In 1878, the armies of the tsar actually advanced into the periphery of the Ottoman capital. The Treaty of San Stefano/Yeşilköy (now the site of the main Istanbul airport) aimed to establish a Greater Bulgarian principality that would have been a satellite state of the tsar in the immediate vicinity of the Ottoman capital. This was unacceptable to the other great powers, and a revision providing for a greatly reduced Bulgaria was introduced at the Congress of Berlin in the same year.

By the end of the century, when war was being waged between Greece and the Ottoman Empire, the English government had given up its opposition to the division of the empire. Since the Ottomans won this war, however, drastic measures were put off for the time being. In 1908, a new series of complications ensued when Austria-Hungary annexed the provinces of Bosnia and Herzegovina, which had been occupied since 1878. This act gave rise to lasting hostilities in Istanbul, as these territories, with their largely Muslim population, had been Ottoman possessions since the 1400s, but also in Belgrade, where the government hoped to annex a large group of people speaking a language closely related to Serbian. Moreover, the Kingdom of Serbia could count on the support of Russia in this matter. These conflicting interests had a significant role in the formation of European alliances when World War I was fought just a few years later.

In many cases, Ottoman territorial losses were coupled with expulsions and emigration. Some Muslims emigrated in a reasonably orderly fashion, but many more had to flee due to acts of war and massacres of the Muslim population, which were part and parcel of the wars of independence in the Balkans. Entire populations, such as the Circassians, were forced to emigrate after the annexation of their territory by the Russians in 1863. The refugees often lost everything they owned; they lived in Istanbul, generally in deplorable conditions and racked by disease, until the Ottoman government was able to provide them new places to live.

This situation was the backdrop for the so-called Bulgarian Horrors. During a Bulgarian revolt in 1876, numerous Muslims living in the affected area had been massacred. To suppress the revolt, the Ottoman government mobilized irregular troops. These regiments, which consisted in large part of Circassians recently driven over the Russo-Ottoman frontier and traumatized by hunger, epidemics, and expulsion, slipped out of the control of their commanders and killed large numbers of Bulgarians. There are widely divergent estimates as to the number of victims. English and American sources conjectured that about 12,000 to 15,000 people must have fallen victim to this repression. The ensuing press coverage was largely responsible for the conservative English Prime Minister Disraeli's decision to bow to the pressure of the opposition and distance himself from his former ally, the sultan.

Reorganization of the State and the Military (1839-1878)

In 1839 a new proclamation guaranteed all subjects the right to life, property, and honor, and thus redefined the relationship of the ruler to the classes representing the state. This imperial decree marked the beginning of a period of extensive reform from 1839 to 1876 known as the Tanzimat ("reorganization"). The slave-like status of all Ottoman dignitaries apart from the legal and religious scholars (*ulema*) that had prevailed since the 15th century vis-à-vis the sultan was now abolished. In 1856, this decree was supplemented by an additional one that retained Islam as the state religion but declared the equality of all male subjects under the law, and thereby went a step further in adopting the model provided by the European great powers.

A revision of property law was introduced in 1858. The state's *dominium directum* (formal ownership right) over meadows and fields remained in place; owners who did not use their land might find that it was subject to confiscation. In all other instances, however, possession rights over state land (*miri*) were made to resemble private ownership (*mülk*). The aim of this revision was to reduce the multitude of legal claims to the same piece of land and thus to give new impetus to the property market. The idea was also that the free negotiability of land would lead to better use. In this connection it was also decreed that only single individuals would be recognized as owners. In areas where communal ownership of land was common, such as parts of Syria and for the nomads of southern Anatolia, this regulation had unintended consequences: powerful members of a tribe registered the land in their names, and the remaining members of the community forfeited their rights.

Reforms of this kind were also intended to strengthen non-Muslim subjects' ties to the government of the sultan by opening up opportunities for political participation to their local dignitaries. This policy evoked considerable interest in the Jewish population, which was largely concentrated in Salonika at that time. The Christians in the Balkans were less enthusiastic; when given the choice, most of them opted for the new nation states.

Rulers and Bureaucracy
until 1908

After the death of Sultan Mahmud II in 1839, domestic power devolved to the grand vizier and his ever-increasing numbers of subordinates. This change was facilitated by the gradual establishment of special ministries and by codifying the rules for the training and careers of civil servants. The old rules of promotion by patronage and the unconditional loyalty of the beneficiary to his patron did not disappear, but their purview was increasingly restricted. The grand vizier thus had a modernizing bureaucracy at his disposal, even though the new professional requirements, which included proficiency in French, furthered careers in some ministries more than others.

A group called the Young Ottomans protested vehemently against this power on the part of high bureaucrats who were accountable only to a relatively passive ruler. The writer Namik Kemal, who preached a blend of Islamic values and political and cultural renewal, was regarded as the group's leading exponent. Namik Kemal and his associates are mentioned here not so much because of their achievements in practical political matters as because of the impetus their ideas gave to the Turkish nationalism that arose several decades later.

The crisis that followed the defeats of 1878 culminated in the acceptance of a constitution and the election of a parliament. The constitution reiterated the guarantee of equality to all subjects, thereby checking the attempts of the great powers of Europe to attain more and more privileges for their Christian charges. This process was headed by Midhat Paşa, who had already made a name for himself as a successful and innovation-minded governor.

The new constitution, which the new sultan, Murad V, supported, was short-lived. Murad, who ruled for a mere three months in 1876, suffered a nervous breakdown when confronted with the foreign and domestic demands of the office. After his deposition, Abdülhamid II acceded to the throne (1876-1909). Abdülhamid was an exceptionally controversial sultan. In the area of foreign policy, he succeeded in delaying the dissolution of the Ottoman Empire for several more decades. On the domestic front, his rule was absolute, and the palace was once again the center of power. An ingenious system of reciprocal espionage by current and potential dignitaries was designed to keep the sultan informed about the loyalty of his subordinates, especially of the intellectuals among them. Particularly in his later years, the sultan feared being assassinated to the point that he rarely left his palace in the hills over Beşiktaş.

The fact that Abdülhamid increasingly used Islamic motifs to legitimate his state earned him great loyalty among the Muslim population and several dividends in foreign policy. The Indian Muslims, for example, regarded the caliph, as Abdülhamid liked to be called, as a source of moral support vis-à-vis the English colonial power and the Hindu majority population.

Abdülhamid also adapted to the new situation by attempting to integrate his Arab subjects more fully into the Ottoman body politic. These subjects now made up a far greater proportion of the population than before the losses in the Balkans. Sons of Arab dignitaries were encouraged to complete the sultan's school of public administration and take up new bureaucratic careers. Cadet training was open to them as well. In eastern Anatolia, the sultan focused on the "divide and conquer" principle by exploiting the differences between Armenians and Kurds. The Hamidiye regiments, which consisted of Kurdish irregular soldiers and were ordered to quell Armenian nationalist unrest, contributed in large part to intensifying tensions in eastern Anatolia.

The Tripoli and Balkan Wars (1911-1913)

The period that followed the reintroduction of the constitution in 1908 brought a quick succession of foreign crises, and any hopes for liberalization and domestic peace that many Muslims and non-Muslims had cherished were soon dashed. Apart from Austria-Hungary's annexation of Bosnia, Italy attacked Tripoli, the last Ottoman possession in North Africa, and rapidly occupied the area. As we have seen, major revolts in Kosovo and other territories largely inhabited by Albanians between 1910 and 1912 were followed by an attack on the Balkan provinces in 1912 by a coalition of Greece, Serbia, and Bulgaria. The allied armies conquered Kosovo, and many of the previously rebellious Albanians joined the Ottoman army in a last-ditch effort. The Ottoman forces, however, were disorganized and outnumbered, and they soon were forced to retreat. The coalition armies took Edirne and once again stood just a few miles away from the capital. Moreover, in 1912 Greece annexed the island of Crete, and Greek armies entered Salonika, one of the Empire's most modern cities and the starting point of the Committee for Union and

Progress. At that time, Salonika still held an ethnically mixed population of Jews, Muslims, and Greeks. However, many of the non-Greek inhabitants soon emigrated; many Muslims moved to Istanbul, and others went to the United States and elsewhere.

Since the three Balkan states could not agree on the division of the Macedonian spoils of war, however, another war broke out between them in 1913 which enabled the Ottoman army to reconquer Edirne. The Albanians achieved the sovereignty they had sought. As a result, the Ottoman Empire was essentially pushed back to the European borders of present-day Turkey even before the beginning of the First World War.

Politics and Survival in the Countryside

The retreat of the Ottomans from the former Balkan provinces in the course of the 19th century meant big changes for the farmers and nomads of Anatolia. For one thing, a new existential basis had to be created for exiles and emigrants. For another, it became increasingly necessary to change the regions from which Istanbul received its grain supplies. Most of the grain had come from the coastal areas of present-day Bulgaria and Romania, but now it was brought from Anatolia instead. There were certainly sparsely populated expanses in central Anatolia, used almost exclusively by semi-nomads, that could be put to agricultural use. But the local inhabitants were quite hostile to the reduction of their traditional pastures, and in the face of problems both natural and man-made, quite a few settlers, who in any case were often townspeople, soon left the areas allotted to them. Others went on the offensive, especially the Circassians, who traditionally bore arms, and whose social structure deviated from the traditional norms of Anatolia; this situation may have prompted the Ottoman government to allocate land to some Circassians in the sparsely populated steppe of present-day Jordan. In southern Anatolia, large-scale projects for new settlements also served to provide more agricultural products for both the domestic and the international market;

these pushes for settlement now affected larger numbers of nomads and half-nomads, and the state authority was heavily involved. Later in the 1960s and 1970s the traumatic events connected with forced sedentarization found expression in the stories of Yaşar Kemal.

In spite of it all, the second half of the 19th century was a time of redevelopment in Anatolia. Villages that had been abandoned since about 1600 were repopulated, and former summer pastures were redesigned as permanent settlements. Local administrative centers that were required for these endeavors were established at this time; while the larger urban centers of Anatolia quite often go back to Roman or even pre-Roman antiquity, the network of small towns is mostly a product of the 19th-century settlement process.

Since very few bodies of water in Anatolia are navigable, agriculture was profitable only when there were reasonably priced train connections. Track systems were usually built by foreign companies interested in branch lines to coastal harbors, but these companies were less inclined to build a comprehensive railway system. The financial outlay to construct a railway system placed a great strain on the national budget. For the Ottoman government, military considerations often outweighed economic factors; as a result of these conflicting pressures, no railway network, as opposed to individual lines, was built in Turkey until the early years of the republic. Nevertheless, the completion of the railway link to Ankara in 1892 had a profound impact on the agriculture of northwestern Anatolia. Feeder services were provided by peasant carts and camels. As a result, the economic significance of these animals did not decline during the first stage of railway transport, but actually increased.

Through it all, Anatolia remained a land of small farmers. There were large estates (*çiftlik*), cultivated by paid laborers, in the Aegean area and in the region of Adana, where cotton was grown for the world market, as well as in the southeast, which had a less commercial orientation. Besides the merchants who acquired land as a second source of investment, there were also families that had been powerful since the 17th or 18th century as tax lessees and local magnates in a particular region. Some of these well-established families had acquired land back in the 17th or 18th century (the legality of their acquisitions was not always clear), and had it cultivated by sub-lessees. In the Balkans, especially at the Bulgarian coast of the Black Sea and in Macedonia, large estates were also common; in 1849-50, for example, Bulgarian peasants rebelled against the large estate own-ers in the area of present-day Vidin.[3] It is important to keep in mind, though, that historians of the new Balkan states after 1945 tended to overestimate the number and economic significance of these posses-sions when using national and social arguments against Ottoman rule. In Syria and southeastern Anatolia, the development of large estates was often a result of the reorganization of ownership regulations in the Ottoman Land Law of 1858. But rural economists who studied the region of today's Keban dam in the Anatolian southeast around 1970 found out to their surprise that large landholdings were less prevalent than they had anticipated.

Anatolian agriculture remained vulnerable, especially in times of drought, notably in central Anatolia in 1873-74, when an estimated 250,000 people and a large number of cattle and sheep succumbed to famine. In some places, the number of casualties was far higher than the number of those presumed to have fled. There had already been signs of a catastrophic drought several years earlier, with below-aver-age rainfall over an extended period of time. A lack of transport links played a decisive role in the catastrophe, but quite possibly the gov-ernment's indifference to this remote region was also detrimental: the tax breaks that would have allowed local peasants to form some reserves even in times of mediocre harvests had not been forthcoming.

Ottoman Manufacturers and the Capitalist World Economy

There has been a recent resurgence of a longstanding debate about the economic implications of the independence movement in the Balkans. Until a few years ago, scholars concurred that whatever the weak-nesses of the new Balkan principalities, each carried out important modernization projects. But a new study by Michael Palairet disputes that this was the case in the economic sector.[4] Palairet's study shows that the conditions for the growth of proto-industry in the Ottoman Empire were relatively favorable after the establishment of peace under Mahmud II, because the provinces paid their taxes to the central government and thus had to replenish their monetary holding with the sale of goods. As a result, money was transferred from the center to the provinces that made it possible to pay the next round of taxes. Independence transformed the situation. The market contracted sharply, land was now easier to acquire, and many farmers returned to subsistence farming. One could of course argue that the new nation-states demanded higher taxes from their farmers than the sultan had, and that it became more difficult to avoid paying them. However, the decline of the cities in many autonomous or independent Balkan principalities shows that economic and social development was by no means an automatic consequence of independence.

European observers who reported on Ottoman artisan production in the mid-19th century painted a uniformly bleak picture. The import of European (particularly British) goods took business away from domestic manufacturers of textiles, especially because the customs regime was quite favorable to imported goods. European importers paid only a modest import duty, as stipulated in treaties with their respective governments known as "capitulations." These capitulations that by the mid-19th century had been granted to all the Empire's trading partners constrained the sultan's government in other economic matters as well.

More recent studies prove that Ottoman commerce and artisan production were more varied than they might appear at first glance. Many manufacturers adapted to changing circumstances. Imported thread, for instance, was woven into cloth suited to the needs of the local market. But the new industries often paid low wages. There were instances of machine-breaking, mechanized looms being destroyed, particularly in the carpet industry in western Anatolia. Quite possibly the total Ottoman industrial output in the late 19th century was no less than a century earlier, but this production was now integrated into the world market dominated by Europe, and large amounts of foreign capital were invested in many branches of industry.

All these developments meant that tax revenues remained limited; and the Ottoman government resorted to borrowing to finance infrastructure and also—it must be admitted—the building of luxurious residences for the sultans and their court on the shores of the Bosporus, including the still extant palaces of Dolmabahçe and Çırağan. By and large, however, Ottoman debts resulted from the bonds the government had issued to pay for the modernization of the army and navy after the Crimean War. The guarantees for a specific return on investment that investors in railway lines demanded also put a strain on the budget. These bonds yielded high interest rates, and the accumulation of debt led to state bankruptcy in 1875. Beginning in 1881, a consortium of European financial backers called *Dette ottomane* administered important Ottoman public revenues. Although the Ottoman Empire was never added to a European colonial empire, toward the end of the century its dependency was considerable.

Nationalism among Turks and Non-Turks

In the 19th century, the Ottoman elites initially promoted a loyalty to state and dynasty that transcended ethnic and religious differences. By 1878, however, it had become apparent that at least in the Balkans, this ideology was not working. In the following decades, Sultan Abdülhamid tried to hold together the empire by emphasizing Islamic solidarity. Opposition to his neo-absolutist regime brought the theme of Turkish nationalism to the fore. The economic aspect was of particular importance in this development. The trade bourgeoisie in the Ottoman central provinces consisted in large part of Greeks and Armenians, whose nationalist efforts were directed against the territorial integrity of the Ottoman Empire. One idea under discussion was to have the state help create a Turkish-Muslim bourgeoisie to counterbalance the "foreign" one; in this period the attitude took hold that any given state would promote the interests of the dominant ethnic group/groups living in its territory and more or less wash its hands of those people classified as minorities. Creating a Turkish-Muslim bourgeoisie also was a policy directed against integration into the European world economy; for Christian merchants were regarded as the accomplices in that integration. The first step was to eliminate special rights for foreigners, which inhibited the Ottoman state's freedom of action. This goal was attained during World War I. However, the establishment of a Muslim bourgeoisie with the help of the state did not really take effect until after 1923, in the republican period.

Opposition to Abdülhamid gathered steam in the so-called Committee for Union and Progress, a loose consortium of several groups, but the supporters of this opposition, known as Young Turks, largely shared a fundamentally secular view of the world even though a few religious scholars adhered to the movement as well. Many intellectually-minded supporters were deeply influenced by the materialism of Ludwig Büchner. Léon Cahun's writings about the Turks were also read, while in later years, many supporters of the movement were drawn to the racism then popular in Europe. Besides their secular view of the world, the opposition found common ground in their call for the restoration of the constitution of 1876. Despite the great authority this latter document granted the sultan, the 1908 coup, which forced the ruler to reintroduce the constitution, signified a transition to a constitutional monarchy. The new sultan, Mehmed V Reşat, who followed the deposed Abdülhamid in 1909, had little power beyond signing the bills of his Council of Ministers.

The open nationalism of the Young Turks became a model for other incipient nationalist movements, including groups that had shown little previous interest in this issue, such as many Syrian Arabs. Official insistence on the use of Turkish and perhaps preferential treatment given to Turkish candidates for civil service positions and other jobs apparently led to lingering resentments. But in this region it was the repressive government measures of 1914-18 that de-legitimized Ottoman rule in the long run.

The Press, Theater, and Photography

In the capital, and to a lesser extent in large provincial towns such as Izmir and Salonika, the second half of the 19th century was a period of innovation in the areas of literature and the fine arts. Before and after 1900, a media landscape was rapidly taking shape that featured increasing specialization of individual journals in particular fields. One journal that was originally designed for a general readership, for instance, narrowed its focus to music criticism. This was of course possible only because public concerts and opera performances were an integral part of the cultural life of Istanbul by this time.

The circulation of newspapers and magazines was hampered not only by censorship, but also by low literacy rates and poor distribution. By the time a publication made it to the provinces, the news it contained was often out of date. Many readers relied on the newspapers in coffee houses, which made them accessible to men of modest means, but limited the number of potential buyers. Even so, the newspaper business enabled some entrepreneurs in Istanbul to establish themselves as publishers. In this industry, the market for printed books, apart from textbooks, was quite limited. Many 19th-century booklovers continued to prefer the aesthetic charm of handwritten manuscripts.

Armenians, who generally spoke fluent Ottoman as their second language (it was sometimes even their native language), had a very prominent position in the Istanbul book trade. In 1854, Vartan Paşa, a high-level civil servant, as his title indicates, published the first Ottoman novel that is still known today, a variation on the theme of Romeo and Juliet. The plot revolves around Istanbul Armenians whose different religious denominations set them apart as enemies. Armenian theater professionals had a key role in the development of Ottoman drama, which increased in popularity during the second half of the century. Güllü Agop, the impresario who directed the theater that introduced the public to the plays of Namik Kemal and other outstanding writers of contemporary Ottoman literature in 1870-80, also instituted a training program for correct Ottoman pronunciation and established a commission that was to select suitable plays and adapt them to the exigencies of his stage.

In early photography, there were also a good many foreigners and members of Christian minorities. Prominent photographers included Pascal Sébah, originally from Lebanon, who won several prizes at international exhibitions in Vienna and Paris, and Abdullah Frères, a firm of three related Armenians. They were soon joined by Ottoman officers and former officers who had learned the use of photography in artillery training. The work of Ali Sami, who taught photography at the military school, shows not only scenes of Istanbul street life but also his emphatically "modern" family: both male and female members, all fashionably dressed, were shown with their books and newspapers. Sultan Abdülhamid became an enthusiastic supporter of the new art form, and commissioned lavish albums to highlight the "modern" sides of Ottoman life: schools, hospitals, factories, and of course the omnipresent military. Members of the Ottoman upper class were quite fond of calling cards with portraits, which were in vogue at the end of the 19th century and are today a favored collector's item and a valuable resource for social historians.

"New-Style" Education and Instruction

There was no continuously functioning Ottoman university until 1900. Earlier attempts failed not only because of a lack of qualified teachers and books, but also because many members of the administration mistrusted students, who might prove hostile to the government, as had happened in quite few European countries. By contrast, service academies for future military officers (and, increasingly, for civil officers as well) dated back to the late 18th century. The army engineering school was renowned for its well-rounded curriculum and its publications. The school of administration (Mülkiye) was a leading civil institution that imbued its graduates with a strong esprit de corps. Moreover, students had been sent to France and Belgium for their education since the Tanzimat period, even though the Ottoman authorities were always concerned that these young people might encounter politically radical ideas. French as a language of literary education thus gained importance, in addition to the traditional triad of Arabic, Persian, and Ottoman Turkish.

Well into the second half of the 19th century, however, Ottoman students were inadequately prepared for these institutions of higher education. State-sponsored secondary instruction was slow in emerging. In 1867, an elite secondary school was founded in a former Istanbul palace, which still exists today. The curriculum was adapted from the French *lycée*; the language of instruction was also French, and the faculty included renowned literati. The school was open to members of all religions. But the great majority of those who sought an elementary education still relied on private instruction, local schools teaching the Koran on an elementary level in addition to the "three Rs," and parochial schools, to which Christians had relatively easy access. For in addition to the schools for Greek Orthodox and Gregorian Armenian children, there were others run by Catholic and Evangelical missions. For Jewish students, there was the Alliance Israélite Universelle, a set of schools based in France, which offered a modern practical curriculum.

In the epoch of Abdülhamid, public Muslim elementary and middle schools also received official support, although they were few in number, especially in the provinces. Even in schools supported by the state and not by Muslim pious foundations, religious instruction was strongly emphasized in the early grades. The goal was to educate students to be pious and devoted to the sultan; the Ottomans described this aim as loyalty to "religion and state" in a manner reminiscent of Metternich's "alliance of throne and altar." In largely Shiite provinces such as Iraq, government support of education was used as a means of spreading Sunni Islam; Christian missions provided the model, even though Abdülhamid was otherwise very critical of them. Teacher training seminars rounded out the educational offerings.

The World of Women

For a long time, historians of modern Turkey considered it axiomatic that the political rights and the enhanced educational opportunities for Turkish women after the 1930s were not attained by the actions of the women concerned, and were in fact not even demanded by them. However, feminist-inspired historiography over the past thirty years has shown that this is a crass oversimplification. In Istanbul and several large cities, including some located in today's Syria and Lebanon, groups of women in the late 19th and early 20th centuries advocated better education for girls. Among Arab-language journals, publications addressed to women began to appear in the 1890s. Their editors were typically Christian women; the journalist Labība Hāshim was noted for her distinguished style and gave guest lectures at Cairo University. These female journalists were supported in their efforts by men, who, at least where the Turkish-language press was concerned, wrote a good many essays in women's magazines, usually in a nationalist framework.[5] Nationalist discourses rejected the notion that ignorant women could be suitable "mothers of the nation." Moreover, more and more educated men expected their wives to possess at least a certain degree of schooling. After all, hygiene and nutrition in the everyday life of a family were contingent on female education, to say nothing of the fact that literate men might be familiar with the belles-lettres of the time in which love and the joys of educated conversation were important topics. Widespread interaction with male "allies" explains why women who demanded better educational opportunities emphasized the good of the coming generation and not merely—or even primarily—their own.

One sphere of activity open to educated women was journalism. Fatma Aliye (1862-1936), the daughter of Grand Vizier Ahmed Cevdet Paşa, combined a rather traditional marriage with successful work as a journalist and as an author of popular novels. Halide Edib (later surname: Adıvar, 1884-1964) also wrote newspaper reports and stories that are still widely read today. She was active in Istanbul as a political orator after the collapse of the Ottoman army in 1918, when the city was occupied by the Allies, becoming (as it says on the monument to her memory) the symbolic female figure of the Turkish War of Independence. Sahiba (later surname: Sertel, 1895-1968) began writing for newspapers when she was still in school, and met her husband when they both worked as journalists. The couple became well-known figures in the early republican media landscape after their move from Salonika to Istanbul.

A number of Ottoman Armenian women made names for themselves as actresses. After all, Muslim women were only allowed on the stage after 1923; but in Istanbul, the theater flourished from the 1850s onwards. Ottoman literary theater, as promoted by Namık Kemal and others, thus relied on Armenian female performers, some of whom took special courses in elocution so as to become the models of educated speech that theatrical authors of the time envisaged.

Some women of the Ottoman upper class, both Muslim and Greek, got their first taste of participation in the public sphere by working for charitable organizations. In Salonika during the late 19th and early 20th centuries a charitable association of Greek women gave aid to old people and especially to students. The necessary funds were provided by people like Elissavet Kastritsiou, a rich woman who died in Bucharest in 1862 and left half of her estate to the Greek community schools of Salonika and Jannina.[6] Muslim women worked for the Red Crescent Society (Hilal-i Ahmer, the counterpart to the Red Cross), especially during World War I. As girls' schools were run by females, some women were able to work as teachers; unfortunately, this area is much less well researched than journalistic activity. Clearly these types of work in the public sphere were restricted to a very small group of mostly upper-class women in the late Ottoman era. But the example they set is of great significance for women today.

Disintegration of the Ottoman Empire (late 19th century)

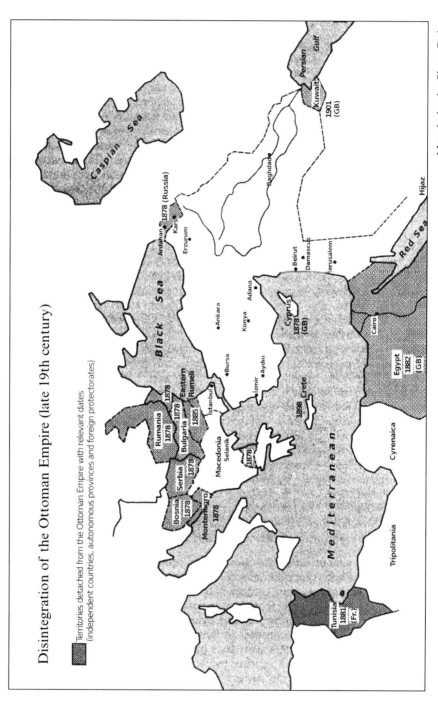

■ Territories detached from the Ottoman Empire with relevant dates
(independent countries, autonomous provinces and foreign protectorates)

Caspian Sea

Black Sea

Ardahan 1878 (Russia)
Kars
Erzurum

Ankara

Bursa

Istanbul

Izmir
Aydın

1878

Eastern Rumeli

Rumania 1878
Bulgaria 1885
Serbia 1878
Bosnia 1878
Montenegro 1878

Macedonia
Selanik

Konya
Adana

Cyprus 1878 (GB)

1898 Crete

Mediterranean

Beirut
Damascus
Jerusalem

Baghdad

Kuwait 1901 (GB)

Persian Gulf

Hijaz

Red Sea

Cairo

Egypt 1882 (GB)

Cyrenaica

Tripolitania

Tunisia 1881 (Fr.)

Map design by Sinan Çetin

CHAPTER 5

◆ ◆ ◆

The Ottoman Military, World War I, and the End of Empire

Military Rule

Significant politicization of the Ottoman officers' corps had already been observed during the reign of Abdülhamid. At this time, quite a few competent commanders esteemed by their subordinates had been appointed to non-command posts or even sent abroad on diplomatic missions, because the sultan feared that they might lend their prestige to a future military rebellion. In fact, the coup d'état or revolution of 1908—the events have been interpreted differently by historians—was partly initiated by the dissatisfaction of officers combating guerillas in Macedonia who felt that they were not given the necessary support (see Ch. 4); certainly soldiers' pay was notoriously in arrears.[1]

During the following years, top-level commanders were closely involved in politics: thus a rebellion in 1909 that aimed at the restoration of Abdülhamid as an absolute ruler was put down by the intervention of a military corps from outside Istanbul. When Italy occupied Tripoli in 1911, many officers accused their government of all too rapidly abandoning the last North African province to the enemy. Several young men who were to play an important role during the World War served with distinction in the small military force that the Ottoman central government was able to send to Tripoli. Here, a circle of politically active officers emerged, of which Enver (later: Enver Paşa, 1881-1922) was the emblematic figure. In 1912 the Committee for Union and Progress suffered a brief setback when Nazım Paşa, the commander of the First Army corps stationed in Istanbul, opposed any activity on its part within the military and the same year, the veteran General Gazi Ahmed Muhtar Paşa formed a cabinet in which the Committee was not represented.

In January 1913, however, after only a few months in office, this government was overthrown when the seat of the Prime Minister was attacked by a detachment of soldiers (*Bab-ı ali baskını*) in which Enver participated. The Minister of War was killed and the so-called "military wing" of the Committee seized power. This coup d'état was a direct consequence of the threat to Edirne (lost in March 1913; see Ch. 4), whose loss many Ottoman officers were not willing to countenance under any circumstances. Mahmud Şevket Paşa, who became the pivotal figure in the new government until his assassination later that year (June 1913), was also a soldier. Moreover military rule did not end once Edirne had been recovered in July 1913 and in fact continued until the very end of World War I. It was after the assassination of Mahmud Şevket Paşa that repression of real and suspected enemies of the Committee began in earnest.

As this account shows, during the Balkan wars and particularly the crucial summer of 1914 the Ottoman government was in the hands of the military. Enver Paşa, who commanded the army, supposedly as a stand-in for the elderly sultan, had also become the key figure in the Ottoman government, along with his colleagues Cemal and Talat Paşa. Yet serious divisions within the officer corps continued; politically active soldiers could be found among the Unionists but also among their opponents. In addition, Enver Paşa had enemies within his own movement. Acrimonious discussions concerning the responsibilities of individual commanders for the recent defeats, and particularly the fall of Edirne, further accentuated divisions.

Another type of tension was structural and long-term, namely the confrontations between officers trained in military schools (*mektepli*) and those who had been commissioned after extended service as non-commissioned officers (*alaylı*). While the former had been trained in the conduct of modern warfare, they were often socially remote from the men they commanded and thus found it difficult to instill confidence. As for the *alaylıs*, while often able to share the concerns of their men and thus to provide effective leadership, their lack of experience with modern weapons was a major drawback, to say nothing of the fact that they often lacked the general education needed for the comprehension of tactics and strategy. Added to the insufficiencies of the communications system – in many cases there were no railroads to bring armies rapidly to the field of battle, and roads were often of poor quality – these divisions within the officer corps explain at least in part the difficulties of late Ottoman armies in the field.

A host of further problems was connected with conscription, which remained highly unpopular, especially when service in remote provinces such as Yemen was involved. The Committee of Union and Progress as a matter of principle had instituted the draft of non-Muslims, which had been on the books since the mid-1800s but rarely applied in practice. Even in 1908, the inclusion of non-Muslims in the army was viewed as a long-term project. At the first stage, men of military age but over twenty-four years old still were excused from active service: they were liable for the exemption fee that previous generations of Jews and Christians also had paid. While Jewish soldiers in particular often served with devotion and distinction during the Balkan wars, refusing the draft and fleeing to foreign countries was frequent, especially among soldiers of Christian and southeastern European backgrounds.[2] Particularly during World War I, the authorities therefore mobilized many non-Muslims not as soldiers but as conscript laborers. As living conditions in the labor corps were often poor and political conflicts in the relevant regions tended to "spill over" into the military, the number of casualties in the labor battalions was quite high.

The German Connection

It was probably the Prussian victory over the armies of Napoleon III in the war of 1870-71 that first attracted the attention of Ottoman military men. A further factor was presumably the lack of any common borders and the absence of the fledgling German navy from the Mediterranean: thus it seemed probable that the newly formed German state (1871) did not aim for territorial acquisitions at Ottoman expense. In spite of limited financial resources, however, the

German ruling group did aim for economic predominance. In the reign of Abdülhamid II (1876-1909), known as the Hamidian period, Ottoman officers were sent to Germany for training in sizeable numbers; and German military missions were sent to the Ottoman Empire.[3]

In 1913 the government of the Kaiser supported the demands of the military for a "revanche" and reconquest of the territories lost in the Balkan war. Arms and ammunition of German make, purchased on credit, helped re-equip the Ottoman army, while a further loan from the same source enabled the government to pay the long overdue salaries of its officials. The debacle of 1912-1913 was not attributed to the German military advisors who had been in place up to that time, but rather to the Ottoman commanders who had disregarded their advice.

In 1913, just when peacetime recruitment patterns were being revised so that Ottoman draftees would do their military service within their regions of origin—as we have seen, this had been a major demand of the Albanian insurgents—a new German military mission was instituted under the command of Otto Liman von Sanders. The latter became inspector of military schools and reorganized the college of Istanbul/Pangaltı according to the German model. He also fortified the defenses of the Bosporus and Dardanelles (often called the Straits in the relevant literature), an act that was violently opposed by Tsarist Russia. Promoted to marshal in the Ottoman army, this officer played a major role throughout World War I.

It has been concluded that in the Great War, the deliveries of German-made arms and military equipment to the Ottomans were modest in quantity when compared to total production in Central Europe. But these supplies certainly enabled the Ottoman armies to hold out longer than would have been possible otherwise. As for the military value of the German officers on active command in the Ottoman army, it is now regarded as less significant than in the past. Liman von Sanders did make a contribution, but his problems in communicating with his fellow Ottoman officers, including Mustafa Kemal Paşa (later: Atatürk, 1881-1938), significantly limited his effective-

ness; he even aroused the opposition of the minister of war Enver
Paşa, otherwise known for his pro-German attitude. Colmar von der
Goltz, the former teacher and mentor of quite a few Ottoman officers, died before he could put his capabilities to full use. By contrast,
the work of staff officers in the planning of campaigns was very valuable, as were the technical services that made locomotives and other
equipment function under often very difficult conditions.[4]

The Ottoman Entry into the War

Conscious of the need for a period of recovery after the wars of 1911-
1913, the Ottoman government approached the Great Powers of the
time for an alliance, even including—rather to his surprise—the
Russian foreign minister Sergei Sazonov, who after all represented the
Ottomans' principal long-term opponent. Thus the alliance with
Germany was not the more or less automatic result of German influence in the military; a first approach by the Ottoman side to the
Kaiser's ambassador Hans von Wangenheim in the summer of 1914
was unsuccessful, as the German government did not believe the
Ottoman armies capable of serious action against the Russians. But
when war actually was declared on August 1, the ambassador, under
pressure from Kaiser Wilhelm, did conclude an alliance with the
Ottoman government.

At the same time, relations with Great Britain were thoroughly
compromised by a fortuitous event: in the summer of 1914 two warships close to completion in British shipyards, which had been paid
for by a public subscription of Ottoman citizens, were confiscated by
Winston Churchill, First Lord of the Admiralty, at the outbreak of
war: historians are divided over the question whether Churchill's
action had any legal basis.[5] On the other hand, two German warships
in the Mediterranean at that time escaped their British pursuers and
arrived in Istanbul on August 10, 1914; they were taken over into the
Ottoman navy for action against the Russian Black Sea fleet, which
was not yet ready for battle. A couple of weeks later, Enver Paşa, with

the support of Admiral Souchon, who commanded the two newly
acquired warships, seems to have placed the remaining members of
the Ottoman government before a fait accompli: an attack on the
Russian Black Sea coast brought the Ottoman Empire into the war
on the side of the Central Powers.

Entry into the war provided the Ottoman government with a long-
awaited opportunity to abolish the so-called capitulations, the rights
of foreigners to be judged by their consuls and the far-reaching
immunities from Ottoman law that these people also enjoyed (see Ch.
4). In addition, the repayment of foreign debts was largely interrupted; as a result, the Ottoman government regained control of the revenue sources that had been at the disposal of its creditors through the
Dette Ottomane ever since the bankruptcy of 1875. These measures
caused a certain amount of dissatisfaction among the Empire's
German and Austro-Hungarian allies; however, on this issue, the latter were not in a position to influence the course of events. Long after
the end of the war, the Republic of Turkey was to take over and pay
off a certain share of this debt; payments were finally terminated in
1944. Other rather smaller shares fell to the "successor states" that
had also once been part of the Ottoman Empire.[6]

The Ottoman armies entered the First World War already in a par-
lous state due to the losses of 1912-13. Even worse, this war was based
on the performance of industrial economies, and some of the Ottoman territories that were most advanced in terms of industry and
infrastructure, such as Salonika, had been lost during recent decades.

Remarkably enough, given the amount of work that has been done
on World War I, there are still quite a few areas where information is
vague. One of the most obvious examples concerns casualty estimates. When discussing the Gallipoli (Çanakkale in Turkish parlance) campaign of 1915, one observer has claimed that there were
about 300,000 Ottoman casualties versus 265,000 on the side of the
Allies. But other sources give considerably lower figures: in one case
210,000 Allied losses correspond to 120,000 Ottoman casualties; by
yet another author we are informed that the Allies lost about 70,000
men and the Ottoman side about 90,000.[7] Some of the discrepancies

may be due to the manner of counting: those men who were ill or wounded but soon returned to their units may or may not have been included. An American military historian working with Turkish and Ottoman sources has concluded that where Ottoman and Allied combatants were concerned, the numbers of dead and wounded were about equal, in the range of 200,000 each.[8]

Other discrepancies involve the evaluation of certain battles: thus most authors consider the confrontation of Sarıkamış between the Russians and Ottomans in the winter of 1914-15 as an unmitigated catastrophe for the Ottomans. But at least one military historian has claimed that from the perspective of the sultan's commanders, the enterprise should be regarded as a qualified success.[9] For a non-specialist in military history it is only possible to record these discrepancies; they show that our data often is much weaker than we would like it to be.

Major Theaters of Conflict

To understand the catastrophes of the war years, events on the northeastern front need to be narrated in some detail. As we have seen, in the late fall of 1914 Enver Paşa ordered a winter campaign against the Russians in the Caucasus, the battle plan being to attack on a broad front in eastern Anatolia, draw the Russians deep into Ottoman territory, and then cut them off from their supply bases by an attack from the rear. However, in this region there were almost no railways, and the few existing roads were impassable during the long and severe winters. Moreover, the troops had not been issued any kind of protective uniforms or equipment. According to western sources, the Ottoman army thus lost over 80,000 men—more than half of the army engaged on this front—within a few months of warfare; 30,000 soldiers died of the cold alone. Ottoman sources record 50,000 casualties.[10] Russian armies entered Erzurum in November 1914 and Trabzon somewhat later.[11]

The Russian invasion encouraged attacks on the part of local

Armenians against the Muslim population. Especially grave was a rebellion of Armenian nationalists in the town of Van, which was occupied by the Russian army with great loss of Muslim life. This was the background for the Ottoman government's order to move the Armenians out of most parts of Anatolia and relocate them in northern Iraq. Settlement was to be at least 40 km from the Baghdad railway, a ruling which limited settlement to arid and infertile areas where it was almost impossible to make a living.[12] Originally conceived as a wartime measure, the government soon reversed its position and ordered the sale of the deportees' property to refugee Muslims. On the road, the deportees were given almost no supplies or protection; sometimes those detailed to guard them made common cause with robbers and other attackers. Mass killings were the result. The number of people that perished through hunger, cold, disease, revenge attacks, and banditry is not exactly known. A figure of 200,000 has been suggested by an American scholar sympathetic to the Turkish position, while a demographic historian has suggested a loss of almost 600,000, and others assume even higher casualties, up to a million and more.[13]

At present this is the most contentious topic of Ottoman history. One point of dispute is whether the government—or perhaps mainly its secret service—had a hand in planning the massacres in order to promote a more homogenous population in Anatolia.[14] On this and related issues, opinions have become so much polarized that no consensus is in sight; and for a non-specialist on the period, informed judgment at present seems impossible. Only at some future date, when the question hopefully will have become less politically loaded, will we gain a clearer picture and view the issue more dispassionately. In any case, it is important to keep in mind that in 1915 parts of eastern Anatolia were in a state of civil war that to some extent had preceded the 1914-15 conflict but was exacerbated by the Russian advance—Russian policy of the time included using Ottoman Armenians for purposes of destabilization and territorial acquisitions—and that the losses of the Muslim population through massacres committed by Armenian bands also were horrific.[15] The observations of two

American observers who visited Bitlis, Van, and Doğubeyazit in the summer of 1919 reflect the devastation that both sides had suffered.[16]

Another significant rebellion involved the Hashemite ruling family in the Hijaz, where the Muslims' Holy Cities of Mecca and Medina are located. Here, outside support for the revolt came from the British, who were concerned about the influence that the caliph, who for centuries had been the Ottoman sultan, might exercise over their own Muslim subjects in India and elsewhere. In fact, Abdülhamid II had made considerable and often successful efforts to promote the prestige of the caliphate among the colonial Muslim subjects of Britain and the Netherlands. In the early days of the war, the Ottoman sultan had issued a call to holy war (jihad), which however had little practical effect in India and elsewhere. At this time British policy planners anticipated that Istanbul and thereby the sultan-caliph would soon fall under Russian control. This consideration was behind their offer to the Sharif Husayn, ruler of Mecca under Ottoman suzerainty, that the caliphate might be transferred to the Holy City if an Arab rebellion against the Ottomans could be brought about. In this case, Sharif Husayn was to become the new caliph. It is impossible to summarize in a few sentences the tortuous negotiations between the various British agents and the ruler of Mecca. Suffice to say that the British never intended to allow this Arabian prince to exercise real power; he was to be a figurehead through which the authorities in London and the colonial bureaucracy under the viceroy of India hoped to rule the area. The military forces at Sharif Husayn's disposal were limited. Even so, the Arab revolt in the desert caused the Ottoman army considerable problems, if only by the interruption of railway lines and the harassment of troops moving through the area.[17]

Until the collapse of Russia in 1917, the Ottoman armies did not score very many successes over the armies of the Tsar. However, against the British and their Dominions, the Ottomans did gain a major strategic victory during the summer of 1915, when the British navy, with considerable army support, attempted a landing. The original idea was to create a diversion from what was viewed as the prin-

cipal theater of war, namely the western front. While this view prevailed, supplying the armies of the Tsar through the Black Sea was
the true purpose of the campaign. However, in the minds of certain
military planners, this enterprise was to serve more ambitious purposes as well: they envisaged occupying Istanbul and perhaps even
winning the war against Germany by a piecemeal defeat of the
Ottoman and Austro-Hungarian Empires. Because the British command did not wish to draw away many troops from the west, the landing was attempted with a limited number of soldiers, many of them
Australians and New Zealanders (ANZACS).[18] A distinguished
British war historian has concluded that even if the landing had succeeded, the enterprise as a whole would probably have failed.[19] After
extremely hard fighting, the Ottoman troops were able to dislodge the
invaders and force them to withdraw; Mustafa Kemal, then a colonel
and corps commander, emerged as the outstanding figure of this
campaign. The battle of Çanakkale/Gallipoli is today a major subject
of historical memory, not only in Turkey but also in Australia, where
the narrative of events connected to the battle has served as a kind of
"foundation myth" of the state, at that time still a very recent political formation.

In addition, the Ottoman armies succeeded in containing a British
invasion of southern Iraq, at least for a time. The invaders reached
the vicinity of Baghdad but were decimated by fighting on the way.
As for the survivors, they took refuge in the fort of Kut al-Amara but
were cut off by the floods of the Tigris and after a lengthy siege were
obliged to surrender to their Ottoman opponents in April 1916.
However, the British took Baghdad in 1917, and late in 1918, after the
armistice had already been concluded, occupied Mosul, a coveted
prize because the region was known to contain oil supplies. Farther
to the west, Cemal Paşa's attempt to seize the Suez Canal in February
1915 was not supported by the local uprising that he had apparently
anticipated. Most of the troops were unable to approach the Canal
and the campaign failed with a considerable loss of Ottoman soldiers.

The collapse of Russia's war effort in 1917 also entailed the break-
away of the empire's Caucasian possessions. For a brief moment, a

Transcaucasian state was formed, but it soon dissolved into the three small republics of Georgia, Armenia, and Azerbaijan. While Azerbaijan was a Muslim state with a largely Shiite population, the other two were Christian. The Germans patronized Georgia in an attempt to gain access to the oilfields of Baku. In Ottoman government circles, there was an inclination to make up for the loss of long-standing possessions in the Balkans and the Arab world with conquests in this region, especially important because of the large local oil resources. It was also hoped that in this way a contact might be established with the Turcophone Muslims of Central Asia. For this purpose, an army was formed which scored some successes. But due to the ultimate victory of the Bolsheviks in Central Asia, these Ottoman attempts to establish a presence in the region failed just as badly as those undertaken by their opponents, the British, who had similar ideas in mind. Moreover, due to rivalry over the Baku oilfields, the Ottoman-German alliance in 1918 was strained to the breaking point.

The Arab revolt was secondary to the advance of regular British troops in Palestine. General Allenby took Jerusalem at the end of 1917 and in the course of the following year advanced steadily northward. But the Ottoman retreat took place in an orderly fashion and the British themselves did not anticipate an end to the war before 1919 or even 1920. That the Ottomans were forced to surrender in late 1918 was not because of any collapse on the Syrian front but because of events farther to the west. First, Bulgaria sued for an armistice, thus compromising the supply of German military material. Shortly afterwards, the Germans were beaten in France, and in November 1918 a revolution swept away the Kaiser and his government. Under these conditions, the Ottomans had little choice, and the armistice of Mudros was concluded on October 31, 1918. The principal Unionists left the country; Enver Paşa continued to chase his dream of establishing a Turkic state in Central Asia. After moving to the fledgling Soviet Union, he seemed at first to go along with the Bolsheviks, but he soon changed over to the anti-Bolshevik side and in 1922 was killed in battle in what is today Tajikistan.

War Financing and the Lives of "Ordinary People"

The sequence of wars that began with the confrontation over Tripoli in 1911 and continued until 1923 completely disrupted Ottoman finances and the livelihoods of ordinary people as well.[20] As the government was concerned about the possible failure of a drive to secure loans for the conduct of war from the citizenry, such an attempt was only made in 1918 under pressure from the German government. The drive was well publicized and even netted the Ottoman exchequer a significant sum during the last year of the war. Financing by means of taxes, by contrast, only covered a small part of expenses. German loans amounted to about 235 million Turkish liras; however, Ottoman war expenditures were largely financed by printing money.[21] As a result, the cost of living rose faster in the Ottoman Empire than among its allies or opponents. An economic historian specializing in the period even has claimed that inflation was introduced into the world's [economic] literature by the Committee of Union and Progress.[22]

Paper money and the concomitant inflation resulted in social upheaval. Receivers of fixed incomes and pensions suffered heavily; and as the public expected the devaluation of the currency to continue, there was a general flight away from money and a concomitant rise in demand for goods in the civilian market, quite apart from enormous war-related government purchases. Even worse, customers not only experienced bottlenecks in essential goods but expected worse hardship in the future: this anticipation encouraged not merely traders but also ordinary consumers to accumulate stocks of whatever commodities became available. As a result, price increases even went far beyond the levels that could have been expected in the face of rising military demand and currency inflation.

Traders were best placed to profit from stockpiling, and those that were in a strong position locally, perhaps because they also operated as money-lenders, obliged their dependents to sell them their small properties against paper currency. These processes resulted in a class of nouveau-riches and a concomitant loss of property among people of modest means. While in pre-war Istanbul people typically had owned their homes, these property sales and the influx of large numbers of refugees resulted in the emergence of a rental market, accompanied by numerous confrontations between landlords and tenants.

Another cause of distress was the difficulty of distributing food and other necessities to the civilian population. While the government entered the war with significant stocks, the interruption of trade with the numerous countries that aligned themselves with the Entente soon resulted in shortages. Wartime speculation included rapid resales of goods that were never consumed but gained in value each time they changed hands. Government attempts to foil speculators by ordering them to sell their wares back to the original owners at the prices they originally had paid for them were at best of limited effectiveness. Rationing was instituted and "official" prices were strictly controlled. But loopholes were numerous and no effective measures were taken against the "black market," partly because the Committee of Union and Progress wanted to establish a Muslim bourgeoisie and regarded war profits as a convenient way of providing candidates with the necessary capital. In addition, some Istanbul guilds were still powerful and generally supported the Committee, so that the government did not wish to alienate them. Those traders that were punished for profiteering thus were often either non-Muslims or people who for one reason or another had fallen afoul of the Committee of Union and Progress.[23]

Market connections between Istanbul and the provinces, problematic even in pre-war times because of the lack of transportation, were interrupted more often than not. Consequently, prices in Anatolian towns were frequently several times higher than those demanded in the capital. On the other hand, farmers were encouraged to increase production by the government's policy of paying primary producers relatively high prices. Many villagers thus were involved in the interregional market economy for the first time; but these economic advances were soon dwarfed by the enormous losses of manpower due to battles, expulsions, and epidemics.

Plans for Dismembering the Ottoman Empire

Plans to divide up Ottoman territories after the eventual fall of the ruling dynasty were certainly not a novelty of the early 1900s, having been made by various opponents of the sultan from the late sixteenth century onwards, and with special frequency during the 1800s. In the course of the First World War such projects once again emerged, this time the brainchild of Allied war planners. On the Russian side, the demand to control Istanbul and the Straits had been voiced many times over; but during the 1800s other European powers, especially Britain, had always rejected proposals of this kind. However, while Russia was an ally in the Great War, in other words until 1917, British politicians now were willing to concede this demand, perhaps in exchange for Russian concessions elsewhere. On the other hand, French colonialist circles demanded a controlling influence in the Ottoman provinces making up Greater Syria. Italy, neutral until 1915, was induced to enter the war on the side of the Entente not only by promises of Austro-Hungarian territory, but also by gains in the eastern Mediterranean. In 1916 a formal agreement was signed between Mark Sykes, who spoke for the British Minister of War Lord Kitchener, and François Georges Picot on behalf of the French Foreign Minister; later on, the French also came to an understanding with Sergei Sazonov of Russia. Differences in details notwithstanding, the three powers through these arrangements demarcated the Ottoman lands that after the war they intended to annex or at least control indirectly.[24]

Moreover, in 1917 the former British Prime Minister Balfour issued a declaration since known by his name that promised British aid in the establishment of a "Jewish homeland" in Palestine. This declaration was made in order to gain support from Zionist organizations; apparently British policy-makers of the time tended towards a somewhat exaggerated notion of Jewish power in the sultans' realm that they hoped to use in order to undermine Ottoman rule – in the early stages of the war they likewise had vastly overestimated the influence of a small number of Jews that were members of the

Committee of Union and Progress.[25] In view of the alliance with Sharif Husayn, the wording of the declaration was intentionally kept vague. In the aftermath of the war, when Britain controlled Palestine, the contradictory promises made to Zionists and Arabs made for a host of political problems.

By the time the war ended, the Sykes-Picot-Sazonov agreement was considered irrelevant both by the British and by the Russians; for the October revolution of 1917 had brought the Bolsheviks to power in the territory that was to become the Soviet Union. The Bolsheviks denounced the imperial ambitions of their predecessors and published the secret treaties and understandings that their predecessors had concluded. As a result, the British government, now hoping for a larger share of the Ottoman booty, no longer felt bound by the agreement.

From Empire to Republic: Anatolia and Istanbul against the Treaty of Sèvres

The set of treaties that ended World War I but singularly failed to bring peace were negotiated between Britain, France, Italy, and the United States. However, the latter government ultimately withdrew from the peace agreement. Many organizations and states—including the sultan's government—sent delegates to plead their respective causes, but these demands were only taken into consideration insofar as it suited the small group of victorious Great Powers. For the most part, the defeated Central Powers were in no condition to continue fighting and could only accept the conditions imposed upon them.

The dismemberment of the Ottoman Empire decreed by the Treaty of Sèvres included the loss of the Arab provinces. This arrangement conformed to the Sykes-Picot-Sazonov agreement but was somewhat modified because of the American President Woodrow Wilson's disapproval of the institution of new colonies. Instead, France received the Syrian provinces apart from Palestine as so-called mandates from the newly formed League of Nations; as we have seen, Palestine was taken over by the British. The difference between colonies and mandates was on the whole minor, but mandates were—in principle at least—intended to be temporary. However, after having driven Sharif Husayn out of the Syrian cities that he previously had been promised, the French government made it fairly clear that it regarded the takeover as permanent.

From the viewpoint of the Ottoman elite, a much more serious loss was the division of the Turkish-speaking area, which had not been occupied by the Allies when the armistice of Mudros was concluded. By the Treaty of Sèvres, territories in eastern Anatolia were awarded to the Republic of Armenia and promises of autonomy were made to the Kurds. In addition, it was foreseen that after a transition period, Izmir would go to the Greeks. France appropriated territories adjacent to its Syrian mandate, particularly Maraş (today: Kahramanmaraş) and Ayntab (today: Gaziantep). Italy was assigned certain Aegean islands, including Rhodes, and the mainland town of Antalya. But the British government seems to have had second thoughts: when in 1919 the Italians did land in Anatolia, the British Prime Minister David Lloyd George encouraged Britain's client state of Greece to occupy Izmir right away in order to forestall any further territorial gains on the part of Italy. The Allies completely occupied Istanbul in March 1920 and remained until 1923. Many non-Muslims welcomed this occupation; the local Greek community even declared that it no longer owed allegiance to the Ottoman government. These events, singularly humiliating for the Muslims, left a legacy of lasting bitterness.[26]

The recently enthroned Sultan Mehmed VI Vahdeddin seems to have accepted his position as an Allied figurehead because he viewed this as the only way to retain his throne. In Anatolia, however, sections of the former Ottoman army were still intact. In the spring of 1919 Mustafa Kemal Paşa, the victor of Gallipoli who was largely responsible for the orderly Ottoman retreat through Syria in 1918, was given a mandate to use these troops in order to suppress the banditry, both political and non-political, that was rife in many parts of Anatolia during that period. The date of his landing in Samsun

(May 19, 1919) is today celebrated as the beginning of the struggle for a Turkish national state.

A degree of political organization was also present in postwar Anatolia; while the government of Enver, Cemal, and Talat had disappeared, the "Unionist factor" was still a force to be reckoned with in many Anatolian towns.[27] Local societies "for the defense of rights" that organized resistance against the Treaty of Sèvres were typically created and run by former Unionists. However, because in the country as a whole the Committee was widely regarded as responsible for the recent lost war, and also to facilitate future relations with the major Allies, the delegates assembled at a founding congress in Sivas in 1919 swore that they would not revive the Committee of Union and Progress.

In this assembly and others of similar purpose held at this time, in which Mustafa Kemal Paşa took on the key role, the delegates agreed on the demand for an independent state within the borders of what had been Ottoman territory not occupied by the Allies at the time of the Mudros armistice.[28] Later in 1919 Mustafa Kemal Paşa and his closest collaborators, now often known as the Nationalists, established themselves in Ankara, which in 1923 became the capital of the newly founded Republic of Turkey.

In January 1920 the last Ottoman parliament began its work in Istanbul: the largely Muslim voters returned a body that was overwhelmingly in favor of the Nationalists and out of sympathy with Sultan Vahdeddin. This split between the monarch and the politically minded elite made it possible for officials technically in the service of the sultan to give assistance to what had become the de facto government in Ankara. Even after the delegates assembled in this town had declared themselves the National Assembly in April 1920 and thereby embarked on a collision course with the sultan, unofficial cooperation between certain administrators of both sides continued. As for Sultan Vahdeddin, he was adamant in his opposition to the Nationalists, and quite a few rebellions in Anatolia against the rule of the National Assembly were undertaken in the name of the sultan-caliph. However, to placate conservative adherents of the sultanate in

Anatolia, the National Assembly steadfastly claimed to be acting in the name of the monarch, no longer a free agent because of the Allied occupation. Therefore speakers of the National Assembly were able to argue that the ruler's condemnation of their actions was not to be taken seriously. This contradiction was only resolved when Sultan Vahdettin went into exile in November 1922. A year later, in October 1923, the sultanate was abolished and the republic instituted; at the same time, the British finally evacuated Istanbul.

The Wars in Anatolia and the
Greco-Turkish Population Exchange

The Allies thus were unable to enforce the Treaty of Sèvres without major armed intervention. In addition, the Italian government was not convinced that its best interests were served by such a policy.[29] Both Britain and France were exhausted by the war and unable to pay large bodies of troops, and the latter demanded demobilization at the earliest opportunity. Given this situation, the Italian government soon sought to come to an understanding with the Nationalists, with whom economic relations might be instituted in the future. Italian troops accordingly pulled out of Antalya, and in the fall of 1921 the French followed suit, evacuating Maraş and Ayntab.

On the eastern border, the Nationalist government, at war with Armenia over the territory that the latter state had been promised by the Allies, reached an agreement with the Soviet Union; for the Bolshevik government was intent on regaining Armenia, Georgia, and Azerbaijan, which, as we have seen, had previously declared independence. A pact concluded between the Ankara government and the Soviet Union in March 1921 netted the Nationalists money and supplies that could be used on the eastern front against Armenia. But just as importantly, through this treaty the government of the National Assembly gained international recognition by a major power for the first time. At the end of the Caucasian war, the borders with Armenia were determined by agreements concluded in the towns of Kars and

Gümrü in October and December 1921, respectively; they are valid to the present day.[30]

Fighting in the west was much more prolonged and serious. In June 1920 Greek troops left Izmir, aiming at further conquests in Anatolia. In this military adventure the Prime Minister Venizelos had the support of his British colleague David Lloyd George. But Venizelos was voted out of office, and it fell to his successor to take responsibility for the ensuing defeat. While Greek troops were within a few miles of Ankara in 1921, they were driven off by the Turkish army in a series of battles and suffered the decisive defeat in August 1922. A few days later, in September 1922, the Greek troops were back at their starting point in Izmir. The war was fought with much brutality: the destruction of villages and massacres of civilians were commonplace occurrences; and after the Nationalist takeover, a fire devastated mainly the non-Muslim parts of Izmir, leaving one of the formerly most active and thriving cities of the now defunct Empire a mere smoking ruin.[31]

It was against this background of mutual hatred that the Treaty of Lausanne (July 14, 1923), which finally concluded the series of wars that had plagued the inhabitants of Thrace, Istanbul, and Anatolia since 1911, stipulated a compulsory exchange of populations between Turkey and Greece. Muslim refugees had left Greece and quite a few Greeks had fled Anatolia "on their own" especially in the days before Mustafa Kemal Paşa's army entered Izmir. Now the remainder were also obliged to leave. Greece was saddled with approximately 1.1 million immigrants, while about 380,000 refugees arrived in Turkey. In what might be viewed as a throwback to Ottoman times, religion, rather than language or cultural identity, was deemed the criterion by which the authorities determined who had to leave. Thus at a late stage of the negotiations, the Orthodox Karamanlıs were included in the exchange even though they spoke Turkish as their native language; and the same procedure was applied to Greek-speaking Cretan Muslims.[32]

Many of the new arrivals in both cases were completely destitute, and for several decades the loss of the non-Muslim populations hampered the development of trade and crafts in Anatolia. In Greece, refugees from the same region were encouraged to form new communities whose names were often reminiscent of the places the refugees had left; and state aid to the newcomers was financed by foreign loans. In Turkey, by contrast, such loans were on the whole avoided; in addition, building a homogenous nation was a priority, and the newcomers were thus directed to whatever town quarters and villages had been vacated by the Greeks. For several decades, immigrants from Balkan countries typically had a higher degree of schooling than many locals, and thus some of them were able to build careers in the professions. Memories of the "old country," however, were relegated to the private sphere; and there they have remained.[33]

In Lieu of a Conclusion: Continuities and New Beginnings

onsonant with the radical modernizing project of Mustafa Kemal Paşa, soon to be known as Atatürk, the proclamation of the republic in 1923 was, for a considerable time, viewed as a clean break with the past, not only by politicians but also by historians. The transition to the Latin alphabet in 1928, the expansion of schooling, the restructuring of Istanbul University and the founding of its Ankara counterpart, the vote given to women, who now were able to enter professional life—all these factors were regarded as indications of a new society in the making.

Continuities over Long Periods

On the other hand, some historians born in the 1950s and thus viewing the early republic from a certain distance have concluded that the continuities between the late Ottoman Empire and the early republic are more significant than the differences. A social and economic historian of Marxian inspiration has even proposed that a strong thread of continuity connects Byzantine, Ottoman, and early republican history.[1] The two empires both experienced periods of centralization and decentralization; but the fundamental socio-political setup—relations of production in the author's terminology—did not change. In both cases, a central administration consisting of military men, bureaucrats, and officers of the palace taxed the peasants and attempted to keep local aristocrats or notables under control. Traders and artisans, while not unimportant as purveyors and producers of goods, were never able to challenge either the central government or local power-brokers. A transition to capitalism was thus out of the question in either case.

From this perspective, the early republic did not bring any dramatic change: on the contrary, due to the disappearance of the non-Muslim bourgeoisie of the late Ottoman Empire, officials and military men dominated the life of the country without significant challenges until the period following World War II. After all, the world economic crisis of the 1930s and the Second World War greatly impeded trade. A low degree of integration into the market, in turn, meant widespread poverty made worse by the fact that the country had not yet been able to compensate for the exodus of entrepreneurial talent before, during, and after the First World War. Only in the 1950s, after the single party system had been dismantled and the newly formed bourgeoisie, both urban and rural, was able to make its voice heard politically, was there a "real" transition into the modern world. Doubtless, this perspective was inspired by the much fuller integration into the world market that Turkey experienced after 1980, when the author conceived his study.

On a more short-term political level, the continuity problem has been tackled by a researcher studying the Committee of Union and Progress.[2] Here, the continuities in terms of personnel form the crucial issue: as we have seen, the provincial cadres whose mobilization made military victory in Anatolia and revision of the Sèvres treaty possible quite often had been involved to some extent with the Committee of Union and Progress. Given the narrow basis for political participation in the late Ottoman Empire, it could scarcely have been otherwise. These men had quite often benefited materially from the war and could only hope to hold on to their gains if the Nationalists were able to take power.

On the other hand, it is important to avoid over-simplification: we have seen that in the Sivas congress the delegates swore that they would not revive the Committee. Moreover, shortly after the republic had been established, the Kemalist group, now securely in power, divested itself from a number of former Committee members through a series of show trials.[3] These latter events were in fact instrumental in making historians wonder about the specific relationship between Unionists and Kemalists. If viewed in this light, continuity and contradiction thus are closely intertwined.

Modernity, No Brainchild of the Early Republic: The Re-valuation of Sultan Abdülhamid

Mostly undertaken in the 1980s, other studies emphasized that significant steps towards modernity had already been carried out in the late nineteenth century. In this period a few regions of the Empire experienced significant population growth—a fact often forgotten because the wars and expulsions of 1911-1923 largely nullified its effects. Trade expanded and artisan producers, far from disappearing, often adapted to the changing conditions of the world market, albeit at the price of long hours and minimal wages.[4] Although the Ottoman Empire was not well supplied with railways, enough of them had been built by century's end to encourage agriculture in western Anatolia by allowing producers access to the Istanbul market. Educational opportunities also expanded, as modern schools were founded to train officers, administrators, and professional men, although non-Muslims tended to benefit more from these advantages than Muslims did.

In addition, the state apparatus was overhauled: even if bureaucratic inefficiency remained a common problem, many aspects of the legal system had been changed in order to facilitate trade, with the institution of private property in land a crucial factor. In the second half of the nineteenth century modern-style urban administrations were founded not only in big cities like Istanbul, Izmir, and Salonika, but also in some small Anatolian towns.[5] While often limited in their endeavors by lack of funds, the councilmen who administered these places raised money for urban improvements like street widening and paving, for public construction in general, and for fire-fighting. Now that many sections of the nineteenth-century Ottoman archives have become accessible, their efforts are more widely appreciated than they were thirty years ago. Recent studies of Ottoman towns in the late 1800s and early 1900s have also discussed the crucial question of agency: to what extent were reforms imposed by governors and edicts from the center, and to what extent were local elites and sometimes even artisans able to contribute toward determining the shape that their home towns were to take?

Even feminist historians have submitted some positive findings concerning the situation of women in the years before and after 1900. Certainly it would be difficult to claim that the Hamidian regime, or the Committee of Union and Progress for that matter, did much to enhance the status of women. Even under the Unionists, rhetoric trumped action; schools for girls always lagged far behind those for boys. Yet historians of the press have pointed out that contrary to the widespread assumption that Turkish women did not struggle for their rights but were simply granted them during the early republic as part of the modernizing "package," around 1900 a small but active minority of women did campaign for education and a role in the public domain. However, because the modernizing package was put together by men, they were obliged to be circumspect in their demands. Very often it seemed more effective to advocate education so as to further the health and safety of future generations.

As a result of these studies, the reign of Sultan Abdülhamid II, previously abhorred by most authors of even moderately liberal persuasions, has received some belated recognition.[6] While the stultifying effects of censorship upon literature and intellectual life in general are acknowledged, the use of religion as a means of building solidarity is no longer regarded as incompatible with a modernizing project. Thus recent historians have come to regard Abdülhamid's attempts to strengthen the Empire by establishing contact with Muslims under colonial domination as a viable effort, especially where India is concerned. The sultans interest in modernizing projects also has emerged, in rather a backhanded way, from his attempts to promote conversion to Sunnite "right belief" among his subjects in Iraq in order to make attempts at subversion more difficult: for the tactics applied in this campaign owed something to those of Christian missionaries, otherwise Abdülhamid's *bête noire*.[7]

Art and Culture in the "Modernity" Project
of the Late Ottoman Empire

Historians of art have made a particular contribution to the reassessment of late Ottoman modernity. In part, this move is connected to the fact that the architecture of the Belle Époque is now esteemed by many post-modernists; as a result, buildings in the eclectic/historicist style of the Hamidian period in Istanbul have also been regarded as worthy of protection. In addition, the sultan was a patron of photography and photographers; these works are now viewed not merely as historical documents but also as important cultural contributions. Thus this ruler has enjoyed some reflected prestige because he sponsored the works of artists, including the Armenian family of photographers known as Abdullah Frères.

Furthermore, the publication of memoirs by numerous figures born into elite families during the early 1900s has demonstrated that during that period many upper-class Ottoman Muslims were widely traveled, had visited European countries at length, and possessed a good grasp of the realities of the societies they had visited. But the wars of 1911-1923, the world economic crisis, and World War II and its aftermath produced a generation many of whose members regarded travel and the concomitant knowledge of foreign languages and the world at large as strange and somewhat objectionable luxuries. The renewed emergence of a cosmopolitan outlook has probably made us more sensitive to such issues. Children of Turkish workers educated in European countries, but also scholars, artists, and others who have spent a considerable portion of their lives abroad, all have connections to relatives, friends, and colleagues outside of Turkey. The strident nationalism which can be observed in other sections of present-day society may well be at least in part a reaction to such (re)emerging cosmopolitanism: the historian will soon discover that a comparable conflict existed at the time of the Committee of Union and Progress.

But even if we admit strong elements of continuity between late Ottomans and their great-grandchildren of Republican times, there are sharp breaks that must also be taken into account. Language and literature are prominent examples. A journal recently published two translations of Hamlet's famous monologue: while the translation from the 1940s or early 1950s is perfectly comprehensible to the modern public, that of 1912 appears to have been written in another language. Moreover, it is not only a question of vocabulary: during the forty years that encompass the end of the Ottoman Empire and the early republic, sentence structure also has changed significantly.[8] Literary taste is a related example: while the modern reader of Ottoman poetry needs to reconstruct a whole different world before he/she can appreciate a work of the eighteenth or even nineteenth century, authors who flourished in the 1940s or 1950s still find their reading public without too much difficulty.

Summing Up the Debate: Nostalgia versus Realism

Thus it does not seem reasonable to simply deny discontinuities. But even so, if the re-valuations we have briefly introduced here are at all realistic, the early republic deserves less credit for setting the Ottoman provinces that now form Turkey on the road to modernity than had previously been assumed. However, we must not forget that many achievements of the late nineteenth century disappeared without a trace during the wars that followed. In quite a few cases, people who lived in the 1920s and 1930s thus had to begin all over again; and only half a century later, in the 1970s and 1980s, did historians rediscover the modernizing impulses of the years before and after 1900.

It is interesting to see, however, that the renewed esteem for the Ottoman past does not include sympathy for monarchy. Certainly the artistic contribution of the last caliph Abdülmecid, who developed a second identity as an academic painter, is highly valued today, but that is not a political matter. While members of the Ottoman dynasty are now allowed to live in Turkey, they are not known to the public at large and play no political role.

Certainly the mere passage of time has encouraged the growth of nostalgia: people who have personal memories of the Hamidian period are no longer alive, but the same cannot be said of the early republic. As a result, the difficulties of life in the late 1800s are less present in the public mind than those of the 1930s or 1940s. People choose to remember horse-drawn coaches and ladies with parasols, the celebrated "life in the villa," preferably located on the shores of the Bosporus (*köşk hayatı*). As for the troubles of immigrants, servants, and widows, who made up a large part of Istanbul's population, they have long since been forgotten.

Given this state of affairs, it is only prudent to make allowances for the effects of the nostalgia culture that exists all over the world but is especially pronounced in Istanbul. The renewed prosperity of the city after several decades in limbo has entered the public consciousness largely through its negative effects. Destruction of monuments to allow street widening or new construction, the use of concrete instead of wood as a building material, the often remarkable lack of aesthetic values, and sensitivity to the natural environment in public building projects have all encouraged the glorification of the late 1800s, when supposedly life was simpler and more beautiful. Interestingly, the public discourse about the disadvantages of change in the urban fabric was already well developed before there was much construction in real life, in the 1950s if not earlier. But with prosperity and the gentrification of previously poor town quarters, Istanbul nostalgia for the Belle Époque Ottoman style seems to grow apace.[9]

However, as a female scholar—and the gender component must be taken very seriously—I have doubts that this laudatory discourse really captures reality "on the ground" in the late Ottoman period; and I remain convinced that historians should try to the best of their abilities to keep a distance from nostalgia and fantasy.[10]

CHRONOLOGY

1326	Ottoman conquest of Bursa
1331	Conquest of Iznik (Nicaea)
1352	Beginning of the Ottoman conquests in Thrace
c. 1361	Conquest of Edirne (Adrianople)
1376	Andronicos V crowned as Byzantine emperor with Ottoman aid, hands over Gelibolu (Gallipoli) to the Ottomans
1389	Battle of Kosovo. Death of Sultan Murad I; Sultan Bayezid I accedes to the throne
1389-92	Ottoman conquest of numerous small Anatolian principalities
1396	Bayezid I defeats European Crusader army near Nicopolis
1398	Ottoman conquest of the Bulgarian principality of Vidin
1402	Bayezid I defeated by Timur and taken prisoner. Restoration of the Anatolian principalities
1402-13	Interregnum; the sons of Bayezid I fight each other for the Ottoman throne
1430	Ottoman conquest of Salonika (Thessaloniki), formerly Byzantine and recently handed over to the Venetians
1444	Defeat of European coalition army near Varna
1451-81	(Second) sultanate of Mehmed II, "The Conqueror"
1453	Conquest of Constantinople (Istanbul) by Mehmed II
1460-64	Ottoman conquest of the Peloponnesus
1468-74	Definitive conquest of the central Anatolian principality of Karaman
1470	Completion by Mehmed the Conqueror of a major complex of mosque, theological colleges, and other charities in

169

	Istanbul, in the urban quarter today known as Fatih (meaning "Conqueror")
1473	Mehmed II's defeat of Uzun Hasan, ruler of the Ak Koyunlu
1483	A struggle for the throne between Bayezid II (r. 1481-1512) and Prince Cem ends with Cem's flight to Rhodes
1484-91	War between Ottomans and Mamluks
1500-04	Shah Ismail consolidates his power in Iran and Iraq
1514	Selim I defeats Shah Ismail at Çaldıran (Iran); short-lived Ottoman occupation of Tabriz
1516-17	Ottoman conquest of Syria and Egypt; end of the Mamluk sultanate. Mecca and Medina become Ottoman cities
1521	Conquest of Belgrade, until then the southern border fortress of the kingdom of Hungary
1522	Conquest of Rhodes, previously occupied by the Order of St. John
1526-41	Battle of Mohács. Hungary becomes an Ottoman province
1529	First siege of Vienna
1543	Capture of Nice by French-Ottoman fleet
1551	Conquest of Tripoli (Lybia)
1556	Completion of the Süleyman Mosque along with the adjacent schools and other charities (Istanbul)
1570-73	Ottoman conquest of Cyprus
1571	Defeat of the Ottoman fleet at Lepanto
1574	Third (and final) conquest of Tunis
1574	Completion of the Selimiye Mosque (Edirne)
1578-90	War with Iran
1593-1606	Ottoman-Habsburg War ("Long War") in Hungary
1596	Ottoman victory near Mezökeresztes
1617	Completion of the Sultan Ahmed Mosque (Istanbul)
1623	Conquest of Ottoman Baghdad by Shah Abbas of Iran

1638	Campaign of Murad IV against the Shah; reconquest of Baghdad
1645-69	Ottoman conquest of Crete
1656-61	Grand Vizierate of Mehmed Köprülü
1660-64	Ottoman-Habsburg War
1661-76	Grand Vizierate of Fazil Ahmed Köprülü
1663	Defeat of Ottoman troops near St. Gotthard/Raab
1672	Ottoman conquest of Kamieniecz-Podolsk (greatest territorial extent of the empire)
1681	Friede of Radzin; a no-man's-land divides Russian from Ottoman territory
1683	Second siege of Vienna
1686	Habsburg conquest of Buda (present-day Budapest)
1687	Venetian attacks on Ottoman territory in Greece; destruction of the Parthenon. Deposition of Mehmed IV
1697	Defeat of the Ottomans near Zenta
1703	Deposition of Sultan Mustafa II
1703-30	Reign of Sultan Ahmed III; height of courtly elegance in the so-called Tulip Age
1705	Beginning of autonomy of Tunis under a local dynasty
1716-18	Habsburg-Ottoman War
1720	Recovery of the Peloponnesus, previously occupied by the Venetians
1725-83	The 'Azm rule Damascus as local potentates
1755	Completion of the Nuruosmaniye Mosque (Istanbul)
1763-73	The Mamluk lord (bey) Ali al-Kabir controls Egypt
1768-74	Russo-Ottoman War, which ends with the Treaty of Küçük Kaynarca, results in heavy losses for the Ottomans
1783	Tsarina Catharina II annexes the Crimea
1788-1822	Tepedelenli Ali Paşa controls a large portion of the western Balkans

1791	Selim III creates a new army corps, known as the "New Order"
1798	Napoleon's invasion of Egypt
1807	Deposition of Selim III following a janissary revolt
1808-39	Government of Mahmud II; he breaks the power of numerous local rulers in the Balkans and in Anatolia
1821-30	Greek revolt crushed by the troops of Mehmed Ali/ Muhammad Ali Pasha, governor of Egypt. The European great powers, however, install a Greek state on the Peloponnese and Attica
1826	Mahmud II destroys the janissaries. Formation of a new army corps, the "Victorious Soldiers of Muhammad"
1828-29	Russo-Ottoman War
1830	Recognition of Serbia as an autonomous principality
1831	The troops of Mehmed Ali Pasha, now in rebellion against the sultan, reach the town of Kütahya in western Anatolia
1833	Russians offer military assistance to the Ottomans. Treaty of Hünkâr İskelesi
1839	Ottoman troops defeated by Mehmed Ali's troops at Nizip
1839	Edict of Gülhane: Tanzimat era begins
1840	Mehmed Ali is forced by the intervention of the European great powers to once again recognize the Ottoman sultan as his sovereign
1853-56	Crimean War
1856	Second Tanzimat Edict ends the legal privileges of the Muslims
1876-77	First Ottoman constitution; soon suspended by Abdülhamid II
1878	Russian troops reach the suburbs of Istanbul; Treaty of San Stefano; Congress of Berlin: creation of an autonomous principality of Bulgaria

1897	Greek-Ottoman War ends with Ottoman victory
1908	"Young Turk" revolt forces Abdülhamid II to restore the constitution
1909	After a failed anti-constitutional revolt, deposition of Abdülhamid
1911	Occupation of Tripoli by Italy
1912-13	First Balkan War: Serbia, Montenegro, Greece, and Bulgaria capture Macedonia and Edirne
1913	Second Balkan War; Ottoman re-conquest of Edirne
1914	Participation in World War I on the side of the Central Powers; heavy losses at Sarıkamış
1915	Successful defense of Gallipoli (Çanakkale in Turkish parlance) against British Commonwealth and French troops
1915	Sykes-Picot Agreement to divide the Empire into English and French colonies or spheres of influence
1918	Advance of Ottoman troops in the Caucasus territory; retreat of Ottoman troops in Syria and Palestine; Armistice of Mudros
1920	Division of the Ottoman Empire through the Treaty of Sèvres
1919-22	Greek attack on Western Anatolia; then defeated by Ottoman army corps, reinforced by locally recruited troops under the command of Mustafa Kemal Pasha
1922	Flight of Sultan Mehmed VI Vahdeddin; abolition of the sultanate
1923	Treaty of Lausanne; recognition under international law of the Republic of Turkey; Greco-Turkish population exchange

OTTOMAN SULTANS

(According to Halil Inalcik, *The Ottoman Empire.*
The Classical Age 1300-1600. Some sultans have sobriquets;
in some cases, these are as widely used as the names.)

Osman I (died 1326)

Orhan (1326-1362)

Murad I Hüdavendigâr (1362-1389)

Bayezid I Yıldırım (1389-1402)

civil war among Bayezid's sons until 1413

Mehmed I Kirişçi (1413-1421)

Murad II (1421-1444, 1446-1451)

Mehmed II Fatih (1444-1446, 1451-1481)

Bayezid II Veli (1481-1512)

Selim I Yavuz (1512-1520)

Süleyman Kanuni/Suleiman the Magnificent (1520-1566)

Selim II (1566-1574)

Murad III (1574-1595)

Mehmed III (1595-1603)

Ahmed I (1603-1617)

Mustafa I (1617-1618, 1622-1623)

Osman II Genç (1618-1622)

Murad IV (1623-1640)

İbrahim, Deli (1640-1648)

Mehmed IV Avcı (1648-1687)

Süleyman II (1687-1691)

Ahmed II (1691-1695)

Mustafa II (1695-1703)

Ahmed III (1703-1730)

Mahmud I (1730-1754)

Osman III (1754-1757)

Mustafa IV (1757-1774)

Abdülhamid I (1774-1789)

Selim III (1789-1807)

Mustafa IV (1807-1808)

Mahmud II Adli (1808-1839)

Abdülmecid I (1839-1861)

Abdülaziz (1861 -1876)

Murad V (1876)

Abdülhamid II (1876-1909)

Mehmed V Reşad (1909-1918)

Mehmed VI Vahdeddin (1918-1922)

Abdülmecid II (only caliph, 1922-1923)

NOTES

Acknowledgments (p. vii)

1. Caroline Finkel, *Osman's Dream. The Story of the Ottoman Empire 1300-1923* (London: John Murray, 2006).

Introduction (pp. 1–37)

1. The work of Charles Wilkins on 17th century Aleppo, currently in press, has shown that slaves in that city were in their overwhelming majority Russian-Ukrainian as well as Georgian.
2. Martin Hinds, Victor Menage (eds.), *Qasr Ibrīm in the Ottoman Period: Turkish and Further Arabic Documents* (London, Egypt Exploration Society, 1991), pp. 103-106.
3. Cengiz Orhonlu, *Osmanlı İmparatorluğunun Güney Siyaseti, Habeş Eyaleti* (Istanbul: İ.Ü. Edebiyat Fakültesi, 1974); Salih Özbaran, *Yemen'den Basra'ya Sınırdaki Osmanlı* (Istanbul: Kitap Yayınevi, 2003).
4. Halil Inalcik, "Ottoman Methods of Conquest," *Studia Islamica*, III (1954), pp. 103-129.
5. Abdul-Rahim Abu-Husayn, *Provincial Leaderships in Syria 1575-1650* (Beirut: AUB, 1985).
6. Ariel Salzmann, "An Ancien Régime Revisited: 'Privatization' and Political Economy in the Eighteenth-century Ottoman Empire," *Politics and Society*, XXI (1993) 4: 393-423.
7. Kate Fleet and Maurits H. van den Boogert (eds.), *The Ottoman Capitulations. Text and Context* (Naples/Cambridge: Istituto A. Nallino and Silliter Centre, 2003).
8. Oliver Jens Schmitt, *Levantiner. Lebenswelten und Identitäten einer ethnokonfessionellen Gruppe im osmanischen Reich im „langen 19.*

177

Jahrhundert" (Munich: Südost Europa Institut, 2004); Marie-Carmen Smyrnelis, *Une société hors de soi. Identités et relations sociales à Smyrne aux XVIIIème et XIXème siècles* (Paris, Leuven: Peeters, 2005).

9. Virginia Aksan, *Ottoman Wars 1700-1870. An Empire Besieged* (London, New York: Pearson Longman, 2007), pp. 59-69.

10. The prospective authors are Ali Yaycıoğlu and Esra Danacı for the period of Selim III, and Meinolf Arens, Denise Klein, and Natalia Krolikowska for the khanate of the Crimea, in addition to Alp Yücel Kaya on private property and economic data collection during the Tanzimat. See Huri Islamoğlu (ed.), *Constituting Modernity: Private Property in the East and West* (London and New York: I. B. Tauris, 2004).

11. For a polemical but stimulating discussion of Turkish nationalism in the late Ottoman Empire see Halil Berktay, "Küme Düşme Korkusuna Osmanlı-Türk Reaksyonu," in *Dünyada Türk İmgesi*, ed. Özlem Kumrular (Istanbul: Kitap Yayınevi, 2005), pp. 179-204.

12. Maurus Reinkowski, *Die Dinge der Ordnung. Eine vergleichende. Untersuchung über die osmanische Reformpolitik im 19. Jahrhundert* (Munich: Oldenbourg, 2005).

13. Carter Findley, *Bureaucratic Reform in the Ottoman Empire, The Sublime Porte 1789-1922* (Princeton: Princeton University Press, 1980), p. 85.

14. Ferdan Ergut, *Modern Devlet ve Polis, Osmanlı'dan Cumhuriyet'e Toplumsal Denetimin Diyalektiği* (Istanbul: İletişim, 2004).

15. A Turco-French conference on this issue was held at the University of the Bosporus/Istanbul in January 2008.

16. Compare the recent doctoral theses of Betül Başaran and Cengiz Kırlı.

17. Paper given orally by Cengiz Kırlı, who is preparing an edition.

18. Nora Lafi, *Une ville du Maghreb: Tripoli entre Ancien régime et réformes ottomanes (1795-1911)* (Paris, L'Harmattan, 2002).

19. I owe this information to Erdem Kabadayı, who is about to defend a dissertation on the subject.

20. Donald Quataert, *Miners and the State in the Ottoman Empire, The Zonguldak Coalfield 1822-1920* (New York, Oxford: Berghahn Books, 2006).

21. John Chalcraft, *The Striking Cabbies of Cairo and Other Stories, Crafts and Guilds in Egypt 1863-1914* (Albany NY: SUNY Press, 2004).

22. Fatmagül Demirel, *II. Abdülhamid Döneminde Sansür* (Istanbul: Bağlam Yayınevi, 2007).

23. Yavuz Selim Karakışla, *Women, War and Work in the Ottoman Empire. The Society for the Employment of Ottoman Muslim Women 1916-1923*

(Istanbul: Ottoman Bank Archives and Research Centre, 2005).
24. Zafer Toprak, *İttihad-Terakki ve Cihan Harbı, Savaş Ekonomisi ve Türkiye'de Devletçilik 1914-1918* (İstanbul: Homer Kitabevi, 2003), p. 175.
25. Selçuk Esenbel, "Japanese Perspectives of the Ottoman World," in *The Rising Sun and the Turkish Crescent, New Perspectives on the History of Japanese-Turkish Relations*, ed. by Selçuk Esenbel and Inaba Chiharū (Istanbul: Boğaziçi University Press, 2003), pp. 7-41. I am most grateful to the author for her advice on this section.
26. İsmail Hakkı Uzunçarşılı, *Osmanlı Tarihi*, 4 vols. (Ankara: Türk Tarih Kurumu, reprint 1977, 1982, 1983); Halil Inalcik, *The Ottoman Empire, The Classical Age, 1300-1600* (Weidenfeld & Nicholson, 1973); Stanford J. Shaw, *History of the Ottoman Empire and Modern Turkey*, 2 vols., vol. II coauthored with Ezel Kural Shaw (Cambridge: Cambridge University Press, 1977).
27. Robert Mantran (ed.), *Histoire de l'Empire Ottoman* (Paris: Fayard, 1989); Ekmeleddin İhsanoğlu (ed.), *Osmanlı Devleti ve Medeniyeti Tarihi* (Istanbul: IRSICA, 1994); Halil Inalcik with Donald Quataert (eds.) *An Economic and Social History of the Ottoman Empire, 1300-1914* (Cambridge: Cambridge University Press, 1994); Halil İnalcık and Günsel Renda eds., *Ottoman Civilization*, 2 vols. (Ankara: Ministry of Culture, 2002).
28. Justin McCarthy, *The Ottoman Turks, an Introductory History to 1923* (London: Addison Wesley Longman Ltd., 1997).
29. *The Cambridge History of Turkey* (Cambridge/Engl.: Cambridge University Press, 2006-). Volumes 4 (ed. by Reşat Kasaba) and 1 (ed. by Kate Fleet) are to be published in 2008, while volume 2 is scheduled for 2009. As for volume 3 (ed. by this author) it was published in 2006. Virginia Aksan, *Ottoman Wars 1700-1870* and Caroline Finkel, *Osman's Dream. The Story of the Ottoman Empire 1300-1923* (London: John Murray, 2005).
30. Evliya Çelebi, *Evliya Çelebi Seyahatnamesi, İstanbul Üniversitesi Kütüphanesi Türkçe Yazmalar 5973, Süleymaniye Kütüphanesi Pertev Paşa 462, Süleymaniye Kütüphanesi Hacı Beşir Ağa 452 Numaralı Yazmaların Mukayeseli Transkripsyonu-Dizini*, ed. by Seyit Ali Kahraman, Yücel Dağlı, Robert Dankoff (Istanbul: YKY, 2007).

Chapter 1 (pp. 39–55)

1. Sources differ on Ibn Battuta's year of death.

Chapter 2 (pp. 57–81)

1. The official explanation was that coffee had an intoxicating effect similar to wine, which Islamic religious law forbids. But it appears more likely that the objection was rooted in the sociability of the coffee house,
where it was difficult to monitor what the male residents of the city were
discussing.
2. This expression was used to designate a heterodox group that is still
found today in Anatolia; it is now considered disrespectful and has been
replaced by "Alevi."
3. Seyyidî Alî Reîs, *Le Miroir des pays. Une anabase ottomane à travers
l'Inde et l'Asie centrale*, trans. Jean-Louis Bacqué-Grammont (Paris:
Sindbad, Actes Sud, 1999).
4. See Cornell Fleischer, *Bureaucrat and Intellectual in the Ottoman Empire,
The Historian Mustafa Âli (1541-1600)* (Princeton: Princeton Univ.
Press, 1986), p. 298. As modern as this argumentation sounds, it is in line
with the thinking of many Islamic legal and religious scholars. It was
considered excusable for a man in dire economic straits to limit the number of his children, as long as his wife consented. It is revealing to compare this attitude to a Western practice, still widespread in the Victorian
Age, that a woman with a known susceptibility to tuberculosis would be
expected to endure numerous pregnancies if her "loving" husband so
desired.

Chapter 3 (pp. 83–108)

1. Leslie Peirce, *The Imperial Harem, Women and Sovereignty in the Ottoman Empire* (New York, Oxford: Oxford University Press, 1993).
2. In the mid-15th century, the Ottoman sultans abandoned the custom of
marrying daughters of neighboring rulers. The end of the Anatolian
small principalities contributed to this development, as did the fact that
after 1500, Shiite princesses from Iran were not regarded as suitable can-

didates for marriage because of their religious convictions. Also the organization of the male section of the sultan's palace seems to have provided a model for the harem. Yet even more than the pages who were dependent servitors (*kul*), the women of the harem were subordinate to the ruler, as they had entered the palace as his slaves. Daughters of Indian or central Asian rulers would have had a great deal of difficulty adapting to an organization of this kind.

3. The people discussed here have been chosen because there have been recent monographs about them; Gottfried Hagen, *Ein osmanischer Geograph bei der Arbeit. Entstehung und Gedankenwelt von Katib Celebis Ğihannüma* (Berlin: Klaus Schwarz Verlag, 2003); Robert Dankoff, *The World of Evliya Çelebi* (Leiden: E. J. Brill, 2006).

4. On Kâtib Çelebi's autobiography, see his *The Balance of Truth*, translated by G.L. Lewis (London, 1957).

5. Evliyâ Çelebi, *Evliya Çelebi in Diyarbekir,* ed. and trans. by Martin M. van Bruinessen et al. (Leiden, 1988); this volume contains an exhaustive commentary by a team of Dutch specialists.

6. Albertus Bobovius, *Topkapi, Relation du sérail du Grand Seigneur*, ed. and annotated by Annie Berthier and Stéphane Yérasimos (Paris: Sindbad, Actes Sud, 1999); Cem Behar, *Saklı Mecmua. Ali Ufkî'nin Bibliothèque Nationale de France'taki [Turc 292] Yazması* (Istanbul: Yapı ve Kredi Yayınları, 2008).

7. [Ahmed Resmi] *Des türkischen Gesandten Resmi Ahmed Efendi gesandtschaftliche Berichte von Berlin im Jahre 1763* (Berlin, rpt. 1983); Virginia Aksan, *An Ottoman Statesman in War and Peace, Ahmed Resmi Efendi, 1700-1783* (Leiden: E. J. Brill, 1995).

8. This expression is used to describe a series of illustrations of biblical stories found primarily in churches and intended for people who have no access to books.

9. For a French translation, see Mehmed Efendi, *Le paradis des infidèles, un ambassadeur ottoman en France sous la Régence.* Trans. Julien Claude Galland, annotated by Gilles Veinstein (Paris: François Maspéro-La Découverte, 1981).

10. Andreasyan, Hrand, "Bir Ermeni Kaynağina göre Celali İsyanları" In *Tarih Dergisi*, XIII, 17-18, pp. 27-42.

11. Cengiz Orhonlu, *Osmanlı İmparatorluğunda Aşiretleri İskân Teşebbüsü (1691-1696)* (Istanbul: İstanbul Üniversitesi Edebiyat Fakültesi, 1963).

12. We have very little information at this point about Christian women in the Balkans, but we know somewhat more about the Jewish women of Istanbul, particularly in more recent periods.

Chapter 4 (pp. 109–135)

1. This title has been borrowed from İlber Ortaylı, *İmparatorluğun en Uzun Yüzyılı* (Istanbul: Hil Yayınevi, 1983).
2. Since the events that culminated in the founding of Serbia, Greece, and Bulgaria are discussed in detail in any history of the Balkans, the reader is referred to the literature on this subject, such as Barbara Jelavich, *History of the Balkans, Eighteenth and Nineteenth Centuries* (Cambridge: Cambridge Univ. Press, 1983). For a novel perspective see Noel Malcolm, *Kosovo. A Short History* (New York: Harper Collins, 1999); this book is much wider than the title suggests.
3. Halil İnalcik, *Tanzimat ve Bulgar Meselesi* (Ankara: TTK, 1943).
4. Michael Palairet, *The Balkan Economics, c. 1800-1914, Evolution without Development* (Cambridge: Cambridge University Press, 1997).
5. Only the magazine *Kadınlar* was produced by an all-female group.
6. Meropi Anastassiadou, *Salonique, 1830-1912. Une ville ottomane à l'âge des Réformes* (Leiden: E. J. Brill, 1997), pp. 376-378.

Chapter 5 (pp. 137–158)

1. Odile Moreau, *L'Empire ottoman á l'âge des réformes. Les hommes et les idées du "Nouvel Ordre" militaire 1826-1914* (Paris: Maisonneuve & Larose, 2007).
2. Uğur Gülsoy, *Osmanlı Gayrimüslimlerinin Askerlik Serüveni* (İstanbul: Simurg, 2000).
3. İlber Ortaylı, *Osmanlı İmparatorluğunda Alman Nüfuzu* (reprint Istanbul: Alkim, 2006), pp. 89-108.
4. Edward J. Erickson, *Ordered to Die. A History of the Ottoman Army in the First World War* (Westport, London: Greenwood Press, 2001), pp. 231-235.
5. David Fromkin, *A Peace to End All Peace, The Fall of the Ottoman Empire and the Creation of the Modern Middle East* (New York: Henry Holt & Company, 1989), pp. 56-57 states that there was no legal basis; Hew Strachan, *The First World War* (Simon & Schuster UK Ltd., 2003), p. 105 contends the opposite.

   Throughout, this chapter owes a great deal to Fromkin's narrative; to keep the number of footnotes within bounds, not all statements derived from his study have been documented individually.

6. Stanford Shaw and Ezel Kural Shaw, *History of the Ottoman Empire and Modern Turkey* (Cambridge: Cambridge University Press, 1977), vol. 2 *Reform, Revolution and Republic. The Rise of Modern Turkey 1808-1975*, p. 367.

7. John Keegan, *The First World War* (London: Hutchinson, 1998), p. 268; Justin McCarthy, *The Ottoman Peoples and the End of Empire* (London: Hodder, Arnold, 2001), p. 102; the lowest figures are from Strachan, *The First World War*, p. 120; the author is vague about British losses.

8. Erickson, *Ordered to Die*, p. 94.

9. Erickson, *Ordered to Die*, p. 61.

10. Keegan, *The First World War*; p. 242; Erickson, *Ordered to Die*, p. 60.

11. Keegan, *The First World War*, p. 242.

12. Keegan, *The First World War*, p. 243; McCarthy, *The Ottoman Peoples*, p. 111 records slightly over 800,000 refugee survivors in 1920. See also Erickson, *Ordered to Die*, pp. 95-104.

13. Shaw; History, vol. 2, p. 316; Sina Akşin, *Turkey: from Empire to Revolutionary Republic. The Emergence of the Turkish Nation from 1789 to the Present*, tr. by Dexter H. Mursaloğlu (London: Hurst, 2007), p. 110; Justin McCarthy, *Muslims and Minorities.. The Population of Anatolia and the End of the Empire* (London, New York: New York University Press, 1983), p. 130. Erickson, *Ordered to Die*, p. 104 says "hundreds of thousands." Donald Bloxham, *The Great Game of Genocide. Imperialism, nationalism and the destruction of the Ottoman Armenians* (Oxford: Oxford University Press, 2005), p. 89, "over a million."

14. Caroline Finkel, *Osman's Dream. The Story of the Ottoman Empire 1300-1923* (London: John Murray, 2007), pp. 534-536 focuses on current debates.

15. Bloxham, *The Great Game*, p. 91; McCarthy, *The Ottoman Peoples*, pp. 106-12.

16. McCarthy, *The Ottoman Peoples*, p. 202.

17. Fromkin, *A Peace*, pp. 218-228.

18. On the violent disagreements among politicians and military men concerning the conduct of this campaign, see Fromkin, *A Peace*, pp. 152-165.

19. Keegan, *The First World War*, p. 261.

20. Zafer Toprak, *İttihad-Terakki ve Cihan Harbı, Savaş Ekonomisi ve Türkiye'de Devletçilik 1914-1918* (İstanbul: Homer, 2003), pp. 99-126.

21. Toprak, *İttihad-Terakki*, p. 113.

22. Toprak, İttihad-Terakki, p. 197.
23. Toprak, İttihad-Terakki, pp. 172-175.
24. Fromkin, A Peace, pp. 188-196.
25. Fromkin, A Peace, pp. 41-43.
26. Andrew Mango, Atatürk (London: John Murray, 1999), p. 210.
27. Eric Jan Zürcher, The Unionist Factor. The Role of the Committee of Union and Progress in the Turkish National Movement 1905-1926 (Leiden: Brill, 1984).
28. Mango, Atatürk, p. 245.
29. Nur Bilge Criss, Istanbul under Allied Occupation (Leiden: Brill, 1999), p. 15.
30. Mango, Atatürk, p. 294.
31. Michael Llewellyn Smith, Ionian Vision: Greece in Asia Minor 1919-1922 (London: Allen Lane, 1973).
32. Mango, Atatürk, p. 390; Onur Yıldırım, Diplomacy and Displacement: Reconsidering the Turco-Greek Exchange of Populations, 1922–1934 (New York: Routledge, 2006).
33. Bruce Clark, Twice a Stranger: The Mass Expulsions that Forged Modern Greece and Turkey (London: Granta Boks, 2006).

Conclusion (pp. 159–167)

1. Çağlar Keyder, State and Class in Turkey. A Study in Capitalist Development (London, New York: Verso, 1987).
2. Eric Jan Zürcher; The Unionist Factor. The Role of the Committee of Union and Progress in the Turkish National Movement 1905-1926 (Leiden: Brill, 1984); Şükrü Hanioğlu, A Short History of the Late Ottoman Empire (Princeton: Princeton University Press, 2008) appeared after the present volume had gone to press.
3. Andrew Mango, Atatürk (London: John Murray, 1999), pp. 443-453.
4. Donald Quataert, Ottoman Manufacturing in the Age of the Industrial Revolution (Cambridge: Cambridge University Press, 1993).
5. Zeynep Çelik, The Remaking of Istanbul, Portrait of an Ottoman City in the Nineteenth Century (Seattle, London: University of Washington Press, 1986); Nora Lafi, Une ville du Maghreb entre ancien régime et réformes ottomanes. Genèse des institutions municipales à Tripoli de Barbarie (1795-1911) (Paris: L'Harmattan, 2002); Huri Islamoğlu (ed.),

Constituting Modernity Private Property in the East and West (London: I. B. Tauris, 2004).

6. François Georgeon, *Abdülhamid II. Le sultan calife (1876–1909)* (Paris: Fayard, 2003).

7. Selim Deringil, *The Well-Protected Domains. Ideology and the Legitimation of Power in the Ottoman Empire 1876-1909* (London: I. B. Tauris, 1998), *passim.*

8. Zeki Arıkan, "İstanbul 1912, Hamlet'in temsili," *Toplumsal Tarih,* 170 (February 2008), 56-63.

9. I owe this observation to my colleague Christoph Neumann.

10. Richard J. Evans, *In Defence of History* (London: Granta Books, 1997).

SUGGESTIONS FOR FURTHER READING

The Cambridge History of Turkey, vol. 3 *The Later Ottoman Empire*, ed. by Suraiya Faroqhi (Cambridge: Cambridge University Press, 2006); vol. 4 *Turkey in the Modern World*, ed. by Reşat Kasaba (Cambridge: Cambridge University Press, 2008); vol. 1 *Byzantium-Turkey, 1071-1453* (Cambridge: Cambridge University Press, 2008). (A collective work; unfortunately, vol. 2, encompassing the period of Suleiman, will not come out until 2009-10.)

Davison, Roderic. *Turkey: A Short History*, ed. by Clement Dodd. 3rd ed. (Huntingdon: The Eothen Press, 1998). (Discussion of the earlier Ottoman history is now somewhat outdated, but the book is very informative on the 19th and 20th centuries.)

Faroqhi, Suraiya. *Approaching Ottoman History: An Introduction to the Sources* (Cambridge: Cambridge University Press, 1999). (Discussion of Ottoman and non-Ottoman archives and literature.)

———. *Subjects of the Sultans*, translated by Martin Bott (London: I.B. Tauris, 2000). (Extensive bibliography on the everyday lives of Ottoman townspeople.)

Finkel, Caroline. *Osman's Dream. The Story of the Ottoman Empire 1300-1923* (London: John Murray, 2006). (Both scholarly and readable: the best single-volume history currently in print.)

Hanioğlu, Şükrü. *A Brief History of the Late Ottoman Empire* (Princeton, NJ: Princeton University Press, 2008). (By a connoisseur of the documents left by the Committee of Union and Progress, with an emphasis on intellectual history.)

Hathaway, Jane, with contributions by Karl Barbir. *The Arab Lands under Ottoman Rule, 1516-1800* (Harlow, London: Pearson Longman, 2008). (Wide-ranging survey that includes social and cultural history while emphasizing the Ottoman framework in which provincial history took place.)

187

Howard, Douglas. *The History of Turkey* (Westwood, CT: The Greenwood Press, 2001). (Ottoman "background information" to the history of modern Turkey, which is the major subject of this book; by an author who has done significant work on the early modern period as well.)

Inalcik, Halil. *The Ottoman Empire: The Classical Age 1300-1600*, translated by Norman Itzkowitz and Colin Imber (New York: Praeger Publishers, 1973). (This book, now a classic, has been reissued several times and remains a great introduction; of course, by this time the bibliography is outdated.)

Inalcik, Halil. *The Ottoman Empire, Conquest, Organization and Economy* (London: Variorum Reprints, 1978). (A collection of classic essays by the master of Ottoman history.)

———, with Donald Quataert, eds. *An Economic and Social History of the Ottoman Empire, 1300-1914*. 2 vols. (Cambridge: Cambridge University Press, 1997, for paperback version). (Informative essays by various authors, especially by the two editors, and comprehensive bibliographies.)

Issawi, Charles. *The Economic History of Turkey, 1800-1914* (Chicago: The University of Chicago Press, 1980). (In contrast to the expectations raised by the title, it is not an economic history like that of Owen or Pamuk, but an anthology of primary and secondary sources, the originals of which are often difficult to find.)

Jelavich, Barbara. *History of the Balkans,* vol. I *Eighteenth and Nineteenth Centuries* (Cambridge: Cambridge University Press, 1983). (Comparative account of Habsburg and Ottoman history.)

Kafadar, Cemal. *Between Two Worlds: The Construction of the Ottoman State* (Berkeley: University of California Press, 1995). (Highly recommended; especially effective discussion of the state of research and about the Ottomans and the intellectual history of the 20th century as well.)

Malcolm, Noel. *Kosovo: A Short History* (New York: New York University Press, 1998). (This book is both learned and well written but certainly not short; presents the story from the Albanian viewpoint but invites us to rethink late Ottoman history as a whole.)

Mango, Andrew. *Atatürk* (London: John Murray, 1999). (A "life and times" in the positive sense of the phrase; says a great deal about the history, both cultural and military, of the late Ottoman Empire and the early Republic of Turkey.)

Mantran, Robert, ed. *Histoire de l'Empire ottoman* (Paris: Fayard, 1989). (Essays by several authors. The bibliography focuses especially on the extensive French production; political history emphasized more than in Inalcik and Quataert. Especially strong in the history of the Arab provinces.)

McCarthy, Justin. *The Ottoman Turks: An Introductory History to 1923* (London: Longman, 1997). (A historian of demographics takes into account the otherwise often neglected sufferings of the Muslim population during the dissolution of the Ottoman Empire; unfortunately lacks a bibliography.)

Ortaylı, İlber. *İmparatorluğun en Uzun Yüzyılı* (Istanbul: Hil Yayınevi, 1983). ("The Longest Century of the Empire" refers to the nineteenth; excellent portrayal of the Ottoman upper class.)

Owen, Roger. *The Middle East in the World Economy 1800-1914* (London: Methuen & Co., 1981). (A classic; deals primarily with the Arab provinces. No Ottoman archival sources, but outstanding knowledge of research.)

Pamuk, Şevket. *A Monetary History of the Ottoman Empire* (Cambridge: Cambridge University Press, 2000). (Much wider than the title suggests; a great introduction to Ottoman economic history.)

Quataert, Donald. *The Ottoman Empire, 1700-1922* (Cambridge: Cambridge University Press, 2000). (Late Ottoman history, by a specialist on the social and economic history of the 1800s.)

Sugar, Peter. *Southeastern Europe under Ottoman Rule, 1354-1804* (Seattle: University of Washington Press, 1977). (Pioneering effort: attempts to incorporate cultural history into the study on an equal footing.)

Turan, Şerafettin. *Türk Kültür Tarihi: Türk Kültüründen Türkiye Kültürüne ve Evrenselliğe* (Ankara: Bilgi Yayınevi, 1990). ("Turkish Cultural History: From the culture of the Turkic peoples to the culture of Turkey and to universalism"; as the title indicates, this book tackles the difficult issue of considering the national cultural history as a part of larger contexts.)

Zürcher, Erik Jan. *Turkey: A Modern History* (London: I. B. Tauris, 1993). (Good depiction of the last decades of the Ottoman Empire and the lines of connection between this state and the Republic of Turkey.)

INDEX

ILLUSTRATION CREDITS

MAPS (created by Sinan Çetin). **Page vi:** The Ottoman Empire in the 16th century. **Page 136:** Disintegration of the Ottoman Empire (late 19th century). **CREDITS.** Details from the following images have been used as illustrations in this text. **Cover:** Bayezid at the siege of Nicopolis Castle. Miniature from the first volume of *The Book of Accomplishments*, by Sayyid Lokman. Topkapı Saray Library, Istanbul. **Page i:** The Golden Horn, with the Bayezid mosque and the Serasker's tower in the background. Guardsmen stationed on top of the tower were responsible for reporting fires. **Pages ii and iii:** The port of Galata and the Galata tower viewed from Pera/Beyoğlu, and in the background the Azapkapı and Sülemaniye mosques. The drawing bears the initials WM, but the artist remains unknown. Courtesy of the Institut für die Geschichte und Kultur des Nahen und Mittleren Orients, Ludwig Maximilians-Universität, Munich, Germany. **Introduction:** The mausoleum of Selim II and Aya Sofya/Haghia Sophia, as viewed from the southeast. In the foreground, an Ottoman dignitary rides to the Topkapı Palace located close by. This image is by Zacharias Wehme, a former student of Lucas Cranach Junior (around 1550-1606). **Chapter 1:** Drawing of Mehmed the Conqueror. Artist unknown. **Chapter 2:** The reception of a Venetian envoy by the Mamluk governor of Damascus. This work, by an unknown artist, today hangs in the Louvre. **Chapter 3:** A young falconer. The artist, Levni (d. 1732), was the last major painter of miniatures in the Ottoman Empire. Courtesy of the Topkapı Palace Museum. **Chapter 4:** Ottoman *zaptiye* in the provinces that soon were to become Bulgaria. These men acted as police officers and as all-round administrative authorities. Known for their horsemanship and their military bearing, they were greatly feared by the villagers. From F. Kanitz, *Donau-Bulgarien und der Balkan. Historisch- geographisch- ethnographische Reisestudien aus den Jahren 1860- 1878*, 3 vols. (Leipzig: Hermann Fries, 1875-79), vol. 1, opposite p. 192. **Chapter 5 and Conclusion:** Panorama of the Galata bridge and the newly built business structures in the old city of Istanbul, around 1890. *Panorama de Constantinople, pris de la Tour de Galata par Sébah & Joaillier. Constantinople, ca.1890.* Courtesy of the Institut für die Geschichte und Kultur des Nahen und Mittleren Orients, Ludwig Maximilians-Universität, Munich, Germany.

ABOUT THE AUTHOR
AND TRANSLATOR

S uraiya Faroqhi has taught English (1971-1972) and History at the Middle East Technical University, Ankara (1972-1987), and served as a professor of Ottoman Studies at the Ludwig-Maximilians-Universität in Munich, Federal Republic of Germany (1988-2007). Since her retirement, she has been teaching in the Department of History at Bilgi University in Istanbul. As a visiting scholar she has taught at Harvard University (1984), the University of Minnesota (1998), and Dartmouth College (2007).

Professor Faroqhi's principal publications include: *Der Bektaschi-Orden in Anatolien (vom späten fünfzehnten Jahrhundert bis 1826*, in *Wiener Zeitschrift für die Kunde des Morgenlandes,* Sonderband II (Wien: Verlag des Institutes für Orientalistik der Universität Wien, 1981, translation into Turkish); *Towns and Townsmen of Ottoman Anatolia: Trade, Crafts and Food Production in an Urban Setting* (Cambridge: Cambridge University Press, 1984, translation into Turkish); *Men of Modest Substance: House Owners and House Property in Seventeenth-Century Ankara and Kayseri* (Cambridge: Cambridge University Press, 1987); *Pilgrims and Sultans: The Haj under the Ottomans* (London: I.B. Tauris, 1994, translation into Turkish); *Kultur und Alltag im Osmanischen Reich* (Munich: C.H. Beck, 1995); *Subjects of the Sultan Culture and Daily Life in the Ottoman Empire* (London: I.B. Tauris, 2000, translation into English by Martin Bott; further translations into Turkish, Greek and Croatian, the latter forthcoming this year); *Approaching Ottoman History: An Introduction to the Sources* (Cambridge: Cambridge University Press, 1999, translations into Turkish and Greek); *Subjects of the Sultans: Culture and Daily Life in the Ottoman Empire* (London: I.B. Tauris, 2000, translation into English by Martin Bott; further translations into Turkish, Greek, and Croatian, the latter forthcoming this year); *The Ottoman Empire and the Outside World, 1540s to 1774* (London: I.B. Tauris, 2004, translations into Turkish, Arabic, and Greek, the latter forthcoming this year).

She is also the editor of several collections, including Volume 3 of *The Later Ottoman Empire* of *The Cambridge History of Turkey* (Cambridge: Cambridge University Press, 2006), and *Artisans of Empire: Crafts and Craftspeople under the Ottomans* (London: I.B. Tauris, forthcoming).

Shelley Frisch, who holds a doctorate in German literature from Princeton University, has taught at Columbia University, Haverford College, and Rutgers University, and served as the Executive Editor and Book Review Editor of the *Germanic Review*. She has written and lectured extensively on modern German literature, and has contributed entries to the *American National Biography* and the *Encyclopedia of German Literature*. Her book on the origin of language theories, *The Lure of the Linguistic*, was published in 2004. She has also translated numerous books from the German, including biographies of Nietzsche, Kafka, and Einstein. She serves on the PEN American Center Translation Committee. Shelley Frisch is the 2007 recipient of the Modern Language Association's Aldo and Jeanne Scaglione Translation Prize for a Scholarly Study of Literature.

CPSIA information can be obtained at www.ICGtesting.com
Printed in the USA
BVOW062348220212

283570BV00001B/6/P